Praise for *Number's Up: Cracking the Code of an American Family*

"This engrossing account of a daughter's relentless search for facts about her family reveals fundamental facets of the human condition. *Number's Up* is a provocative book that will transform its readers. A moving testimony, it presents one family's history as the history of what America was, is, and can be—if the nation's inhabitants have the collective will."
—Neil Roberts, coeditor of *Creolizing Hannah Arendt*

"Johnisha Matthews Levi is honest and compassionate and displays a genuine attempt to understand her family and the broader American culture regarding race and incarceration. I enjoyed learning more about her family history and its mysteries and nuances. Reading Levi's book is indeed like cracking a code, and she draws you in and guides you the whole way."
—Monic Ductan, author of *Daughters of Muscadine*

"A beautiful story of love and struggle told with courage and heart by a compelling narrator."
—Paula Blackman, author of *Night Train to Nashville: The Greatest Untold Story of Music City*

"Levi takes readers on an emotional journey as she uncovers and comes to terms with her family's history. Through her brilliant storytelling, Levi crafts a very personal and brutally honest narrative that highlights themes of identity, resilience, forgiveness, and love. She tells a story of hope in the face of uncertainty and provides readers with a book that reveals the human spirit's capacity for healing and growth. *Number's Up* is more than a simple memoir or family history; it is a story of discovery and an intercessory prayer of thanksgiving and grace for an American family."
—Learotha Williams Jr., coeditor of *I'll Take You There: Exploring Nashville's Social Justice Sites*

Number's Up

Number's Up

CRACKING THE CODE OF AN AMERICAN FAMILY

Johnisha Matthews Levi

A note to the reader: This volume contains references to domestic violence, sexual abuse, and other sensitive topics and includes two instances of a racial slur. Discretion is advised.

Copyright © 2025 by Johnisha Matthews Levi

Published by The University Press of Kentucky, scholarly publisher for the Commonwealth, serving Bellarmine University, Berea College, Centre College of Kentucky, Eastern Kentucky University, The Filson Historical Society, Georgetown College, Kentucky Historical Society, Kentucky State University, Morehead State University, Murray State University, Northern Kentucky University, Spalding University, Transylvania University, University of Kentucky, University of Louisville, University of Pikeville, and Western Kentucky University.

All rights reserved.

Editorial and Sales Offices: The University Press of Kentucky
663 South Limestone Street, Lexington, Kentucky 40508-4008
www.kentuckypress.com

Cataloging-in-Publication data available from the Library of Congress

ISBN 978-1-9859-0232-9 (hardcover)
ISBN 978-1-9859-0258-9 (pdf)
ISBN 978-1-9859-0257-2 (epub)

Member of the Association
of University Presses

To Jon, my *bashert*. Thank you for your love
and for your unwavering belief in me.

To my enslaved ancestors Frederick Simms and
Martha Flemons—so that your names may live on.

These energies have always been around. This thing, we term it hustle, but it's really just the ingenuity necessary to survive and navigate in the world. . . . It's still wisdom, it's still knowledge, it's still invention, it's still development, it's still progress. . . . We can acknowledge brilliance in the streets, we can acknowledge soul in the academic space, and we can allow these things to come together.

LAURYN HILL

I pray you, in your letters,
When you shall these unlucky deeds relate,
Speak of me as I am; nothing extenuate.

WILLIAM SHAKESPEARE, *OTHELLO*

Contents

Prologue: Independence Day   *ix*

Part 1   The Gambler

The Homecoming Story   *3*
Visiting Hours   *6*
The Investigation   *13*
The Lottery   *24*
Trouble Man   *29*

Part 2   The Graduate

The Early Years   *41*
Real Estate   *48*
Code-Switching   *54*
South Pacific   *61*
"Father, Father, We Don't Need to Escalate"   *64*
Kingdom Come   *66*
Insufficient Funds   *79*
Hell or High Water   *85*
The Verdict   *87*
Evidence of Things Not Seen   *96*
Graduation Day   *109*
An Imperfect Mind   *115*

viii *Contents*

Part 3 The Guardian

Basic Human Needs *125*
Probation *129*
Spirits in the Material World *133*
Two Weddings *136*
The Protector *144*
Bashert *152*
The Diagnosis *159*
Good-bye *166*
Liberty Crest *173*
Epilogue *178*

Acknowledgments *181*
Notes *183*
Selected Bibliography *191*

Illustrations follow page 86

Prologue
Independence Day

The District of Columbia Board of Parole, having been advised that John Matthews D.C.D.C. 186767 is eligible to be PAROLED, and it being the opinion of the BOARD OF PAROLE that the above named will remain at liberty without violating the law [and] that the release of the individual to supervision is not incompatible with the welfare of society, it is ORDERED by the BOARD that the above named be PAROLED on September 28, 1977.

For four decades, I never questioned the official account of my birth. My bronze skin, my nearly black kinky hair, and my deep-set amber eyes confirmed that I was the biological child of John and Lussia Matthews. According to my mother, she checked herself into Columbia Hospital for Women in Washington, DC, for a cesarean section and delivered me at 5:39 a.m. on August 16, 1977. Four days later, I went home and began my life as the youngest child in a blended family: my Black Catholic father, my white Jewish mother, and my ten half-siblings whose ages spanned three decades.

Over the years, I would periodically take out my "Baby Days" memory album, with its cover design of a pastel-colored quilt. It embodied the "official" version of the story I had often been told; the album, which contained memorabilia from my first six years, also acted as a sort of talisman. I would flip through the collection of Kodaks and Polaroids beneath their plastic overlays and peruse the school merit ribbons, pediatric records, and elementary school

x *Prologue*

report cards. The yellowing papers and fading photographs were lasting and necessary proof of my existence, more so than my own bones, hair, and skin. And so I was convinced that the essential truth of my days stemmed from a handful of ostensibly provable facts—a straight line of cause and effect. However, years after my parents died, I learned there was one big misrepresentation about the day I was born. Suddenly, I watched the story I treasured degrade, much like the colors in the snapshots of my infancy or the spy paper my dad used to record bets as part of his underground gambling operation.

I stumbled onto the truth because I had finally resolved to sort through the boxes containing the bird's nest of photos and documents left behind in my mother's closets and drawers six years after she passed away from ovarian cancer. I tend to procrastinate when it comes to these sorts of chores, but it was the Fourth of July 2021—an extended holiday weekend during the COVID-19 pandemic that left me with many empty hours to fill. Some of the documents I had already encountered as part of the cleaning-out process that routinely follows a family member's death. In addition to the papers, I had kept my mother's massive china collection (which she liked to remind me was worth a lot of money in case of an emergency), her Lenox figurines and miniature enamel Halcyon boxes (the tchotchkes she loved), a few antique lamps, and her black lacquer curio cabinet and folding screen.

My mother was not a hoarder, but it would be fair to describe her as a chaotic archivist. In nothing remotely resembling a filing system, she had retained divorce papers, property deeds, family photos, diplomas, high school and college accolades, and assembly programs, as well as envelopes containing desiccated baby teeth she had collected as the tooth fairy. The oldest documents and photographs were irreversibly and unforgivably creased and stuffed into gift bags and shopping bags.

But it was a single page, folded in uneven quarters and more than a bit bedraggled, that caught my eye for the first time. Its ragged appearance belied its significance, for it granted my father parole from a correctional facility when he was fifty-three years old—and more than a month after I was born. It was my dad's modern-day freedom paper, which, in bewilderment, I now placed alongside the honorable discharge papers from the US Navy that I had seen many times before.

I had previously known the bare minimum, gleaned from innuendo and the whisperings of my parents' friends and my much older siblings—that my dad had served time in the infamous, now-shuttered Lorton Correctional Complex. Once, as an elderly man, he had mentioned his time at Lorton to me in passing. But no one had ever shared any concrete details or a specific timeline. All I knew was that the sentence was related to what the family referred to as "the numbers."

There were many times in my life that I wished my father were gone, but I never imagined him being anywhere but at my mother's side when I was born. This paper created a new, disquieting aperture in my parents' lives before they became my mother and my father, leaving me with a host of questions. Why was my dad being punished? How did my mother feel about the father of her newborn child being incarcerated? How did my father feel being cut off from the large family he had always shepherded? How difficult was it for my mother to wake up every morning and care for a newborn as well as her partner's older but still dependent children? How helpless did my father feel being unable to pay the bills when his family (as well as the community) thought of him as the provider?

In the midst of my shock over this newfound information, I reflected on the story my mother liked to tell about my (now barely visible) facial birthmark. When I was an infant, the birthmark presented as a bright scarlet spot on the right side of my forehead, resembling an off-center bindi. An elderly Chinese lady had told her it was a sign of good fortune and blessing. Perhaps my mom latched on to this story as a type of mantra, hoping it would become a self-fulfilling prophecy for a child born during such an unlucky period in her parents' lives. On my best days, I still believe this. But on my worst days, I see this distinguishing feature as the "fear like a faint line in the center of [my] forehead" from Audre Lorde's poem "A Litany for Survival."

xii *Prologue*

Finding the parole paper also resurrected some long-standing unresolved family issues. My father lived for eighty-eight years, yet as an adult I found him just as inscrutable as I had as a child, as if that short but crucial window of time when we were separated irrevocably estranged us. Equally confounding was the longevity of my parents' relationship. Why did my sane and practical mother bind herself to a mercurial and frequently abusive man until the day he died? These realities isolated me and forced me to hold and guard secrets. My father was gone, but my anger and confusion lived on.

Much like the boxes I had neglected, the circumstances of my father's imprisonment and the essential truths of his legacy were long overdue for inspection. This process would in some ways be simplified by the emotional chasms in the Matthews family. We had begun to unravel well before a woman walking her dog in Rock Creek Park stumbled upon my father's four-week-old corpse. Three of my siblings' lives had been senselessly cut short. Most of the others lived in DC, but holidays and birthday celebrations no longer brought us together. Even a group text was too difficult to sustain. Additionally, the man I grew up with was, in many ways, very different from the young tyrant who had raised my older siblings. In the later years of my childhood, I was essentially an only child, and my parents and I formed a triptych of sorts.

I began my search seeking clarity about my parents' relationships with each other and with me, but I ultimately came to recognize the enormity of a single episode—my father's arrest—in our lives. I would also find in this one family episode the kernels of American history: the violence of segregation, immigration, and incarceration; the harms of co-optation and gentrification; and, undergirding it all, the almighty dollar.

Part 1
THE GAMBLER

The Homecoming Story

The insidious sweetness of the Johnson's baby powder my mother used for my diaper changes still emanates from the pages of my "Baby Days" album. On the page titled "The Homecoming" the following text appears:

> Baby's First Day Home was Sunday Aug. 20
> Daddy & Brothers an[d] Sister was [*sic*] there to help
> Description and Reaction: [blank]
> Photos: [blank]

My mom's inelegant left-slanted handwriting filled in the blanks for the date and the helpers in attendance. Before I discovered my dad's parole paper, I had never given this page more than a glance. I had no reason to question who was present for my homecoming or why the space for photos was blank. Subsequent pages contained many baby pictures that showed my father holding me, sleeping with me, playing with me, making faces at me. But now I had an official document, dated and signed, providing irrefutable proof that something was amiss with the story I had been told.

Between the passing of my father's generation and the rifts in our family, there weren't a lot of people left who could tell me the truth. But I knew I should start with my brother Johnny. At the time of my birth, Johnny was a gangly, gap-toothed sixteen-year-old and a star point guard on the Archbishop Carroll High School basketball team. He lived with my parents in our house on Evarts Street NE after Dad separated from Johnny's mother, Cora. Even when my mother officially became Johnny's stepmother, he continued to call her Ms. Lussia out of respect for his elders. He felt comfortable joking around with my mother, but he also confided in her about his struggles to gain my father's love and approval and his hurt that his own mother wasn't capable of raising him. Now in his early sixties, Johnny is a philosophical, even-keeled girl dad who quotes the arcane wisdom of George Clinton and Parliament Funkadelic when he isn't working IT or slaying it in the kitchen. Johnny and I talk on the phone infrequently, but when we do, we can speak from the heart and without pretense. During the pandemic, we began texting a lot. I had previously avoided that method of communication, but I found myself relying on it more and more for even the most intimate conversations. So I sent Johnny an image of the parole document and texted, "Look what I found in my mom's papers! Does that mean Dad was not even there when I was born?" A small part of me hoped Johnny would tell me there had been a huge misunderstanding. Surely he would be able to unravel the truth and debunk the worst-case scenario. I didn't have to wait long for his response: "Yeah Daddy was still in but he was on his way home." I had to take a beat. What was he saying?

> Me: Well that hurts me for some reason. I know [my mother] wasn't truthful about some of that stuff bc she probably didn't want me to feel bad. Poor Dad. I know that must have been sad for him.
> Johnny: I'm sure it was. He was there in your heart.
> Me: I feel not so bad for me but for both of them.
> Johnny: Find a way to make peace with it. It may take a minute.

Although I'm sure he didn't intend it, Johnny came off as cavalier. I was angry at my dead parents and irritated at him for keeping their secret so many years after the fact.

The Homecoming Story 5

With this startling new information propelling me, I began to turn the pages of my baby album and scrutinize it through a different lens. Perhaps if I had children of my own I would have realized that I look a little more alert than the typical newborn in the first picture of my father holding me. I am splayed out in his arms—my tiny body stretching, my arms extended with my fists balled tight. I seem to be either suppressing or finishing a yawn, with my head turned toward him. In response, he is making a funny face at me, and he is dressed casually (unusual for him) in a short-sleeved red and blue plaid shirt and denim bell bottoms. Wearing a pink velour short set, I look only slightly larger than my seven-pound birth weight. On the back of the photo, my mom scrawled "Oct. '77"—two months after my birth.

It turns out that the true photographs of my homecoming were tucked away in one of the lavender gift bags I had used to distribute my wedding favors. Stuffed in with hundreds of other photos that spanned decades—from my mother's childhood through my high school years—are three darkened Polaroids. I am wearing a frilly white dress with puffy sleeves, my tiny pink feet sticking out. In one photo, my sandy-haired sister Megan, who is seven years my senior, is clutching me, an elfin grin on her face, as she sits on a pristine white baby blanket spread on the sofa. In another photo, my mom, in a flower print dress, is sitting next to Megan. A third photo, posed in a similar fashion, is of me with my teenage brother Charles. He is clearly more adept at holding a baby than my sister, supporting my small body and looking pleased with himself. Megan sits on the floor with some construction paper and markers. My invisible mother is doubtless coaching the handling of her newborn baby. These photos confirmed the truth. If everyone was taking turns holding me and my father had been there, wouldn't there be a similar photo of him? And what exactly was he incarcerated for?

Visiting Hours

As I rummaged through the stacks of photos with a singular focus, I unearthed two more Polaroids I had never seen before. The first must have been taken in the winter or perhaps the early spring, based on the subjects' wardrobes. My father is at the center of the photograph in a denim prison-issue uniform—wide-legged pants and a short-sleeved shirt with a left breast pocket, where he's stuffed his thick-framed black glasses. His face is grooved with strain. My sister Megan, in bright red tights and a matching pinafore, is curled into Dad's left armpit, mugging for the camera. (No matter how miserable she might be on the inside, Megan has always been able to turn it on for the camera.) Mom, wearing a velour or velvet blazer, is turned to the side; she and my brother Charles, who is all scrawny limbs, look appropriately glum. They are posed in front of a blond, wood-paneled wall.

In the second Polaroid with the same background, my mom's pregnancy is beginning to show—in her floral dress (the same one she wore in the homecoming photo), her baby bump is subtle, and her face is fleshier. This is consistent with her boasts throughout the years that she never had to wear maternity clothes until the very end of her pregnancy. My father is unsmiling as he again wraps his arm around my inappropriately gleeful sister. On either side of my parents are Charles and my brother Adrin (who would serve time in Lorton almost twenty years later), their faces blank masks in the poor lighting.

These Polaroids are more than family photographs: they are artifacts of the American carceral state. No doubt a collage of such photos, featuring a disproportionate number of Black and brown inmates, will someday be displayed in a museum as testament to a less enlightened and more brutal era, much like the three-story Tower of Faces, a photography exhibit of Jewish victims and survivors at the US Holocaust Memorial Museum that my mother took me to see in high school. I think of all the families that have similar Polaroids in their closets, the gatherings they portray insufficient substitutes for holidays and birthdays. They capture the aging of both children and parents, as well as their anguish, anger, and loss.

It also dawns on me that something as sacrosanct as naming a child might have occurred during one of these visits. My dad chose the name Johnisha (pronounced Juh-NISH-a) as a way of combining his name and my mom's, Lussia (pronounced LOO-sha). My mother would have preferred to name me something more conventional—Julie, Vanessa, and Alexandra were the top contenders. I don't know if she was taken with the romanticism of the gesture or the uniqueness of the name or if she just wanted to give my dad a bigger role to play, given that he was forced to be an absentee father.

During all the years I spent with my father, he mentioned his time in Lorton only once—when he was in his eighties. He was already in the throes of dementia, and I couldn't be sure whether his recollections were an actual memory or the delusions of an altered mind. "At Lorton," he blurted out, "it was my responsibility to take care of the cows." This is one of many moments that I now look back on and wonder why I didn't ask any questions. Was I afraid, unprepared, or simply distracted? Or was I just so conditioned to not prying into my parents' secrets that I let it go?

The history of Lorton Correctional Complex reflects the history of twentieth-century Washington, DC. The institution opened in 1910 in Virginia as the Occoquan Workhouse for DC prisoners who had committed lesser offenses. In fact, much of what became the modern-era facility was built in the 1930s by the prisoners themselves, including the dormitories, dining hall, laundry, bake shop, ice plant, and hospital. The prisoners made the building bricks, and the lumber came from trees they cut down on the property.

However, in the decades to come, the facility that once exemplified Progressive Era philosophies about prisoner rehabilitation and reformation gave way to a much darker, law-and-order version of penal hell. Lorton was expanded to house prisoners convicted of felonies. Consisting of seven facilities, it ultimately became known "as an oppressive, poorly managed prison where escapes and riots often have made news and guards sometimes have been charged with crimes themselves."[1]

In 1974, three years before my father served time at Lorton, Lorton inmates made the news when they staged a tense, twenty-hour standoff. On Christmas Eve, one hundred inmates took control of the prison's maximum-security section and seized ten guards as hostages. In a related episode, four inmates escaped in a prison guard's vehicle. One of the inmate's bodies was subsequently found in the abandoned car.

By the mid-1990s, Lorton was bursting at the seams, housing nearly 50 percent more prisoners than it could reasonably accommodate without the requisite budget increases. Its more than seven thousand inmates were overwhelmingly Black men.

After years of Virginia politicians fighting to close Lorton, the campaign was ultimately successful, and the land was sold to Fairfax County for redevelopment and historic preservation. The remaining prisoners convicted of felonies were transferred to other facilities in the Federal Bureau of Prisons, and DC residents convicted of felonies are now incarcerated in federal prisons across the nation. And what became of the Lorton campus? It is now lauded by some as an example of adaptive reuse and is the site of a cultural arts center and the ironically named Liberty Crest, an urban village consisting of loft-style apartments, almost two hundred single-family and town homes, a number of retail establishments and restaurants, and collaborative office spaces.

My father's memory of caring for cows at Lorton was not a dementia-induced delusion. Lorton had a working dairy that was part of the prison's agricultural complex, which consisted of orchards and vegetable fields, cattle herds, a turkey ranch, and a slaughterhouse. Although the other components of the prison's large-scale farming operation came to an end in 1972, the dairy remained open for business, and the inmates often put in eight- to fourteen-hour workdays. The *Washington Post* covered a day in the life of Lorton's dairy "farmers," making it sound almost idyllic:

> At 5:22 a.m., after the men have spent a noisy hour hosing and power-scrubbing homogenizers, tanks and floors, the morning's first cow sways into the worn, white building that serves as the milking barn. Others follow, a few of them lowing forlornly with the pain of milk-swelled udders. They soon fill the dozen pens that surround two sunken pits in the middle of the room.
>
> A few minutes later, the unlikely pastoral of cow and convict bursts into a sustained frenzy of activity. Inmates shout and yank the udders of jittery cows; milk tubes whisk the liquid up to the ceiling and into a holding tank in the next room; and at the hurricane's center, unfazed by the noise and swirl, a black cat serenely laps fresh milk from a coffee cup.[2]

When I imagine my father working in a prison dairy, I am slightly bemused at the idea of that elegant man trying to command cows in his favorite shoes—a pair of crocodile Gucci loafers. (These are the same shoes my brothers stole and tried to sell on U Street before they were ratted out by my dad's friends. And yes, they caught hell.) Although he grew up in rural La Plata, Maryland, he worked hard to shed his country-boy ways. He had a closet full of well-tailored designer suits (Armani, Yves St. Laurent, Pierre Cardin, and Raleigh), stylish fedoras, and silk pocket scarves. His color palette was decidedly traditional—he wasn't flamboyant like Adrin, who grew up to wear two-toned saddle shoes, huge houndstooth

10   *The Gambler*

prints, and bright red suspenders. My dad preferred muted pastels for his accessories (lavender, pale pink, and sky blue, along with some darker, more staid tones such as navy). His ties bore miniature geometric or floral patterns—my favorite was a lavender one with pale blue and pink buds. Perhaps his disdain for jeans originated during his time in both Lorton and the US Navy, where the uniforms included denim bell bottoms. "The navy bell bottoms," he explained, "could be transformed into an improvised floating device in case of an emergency."

His attention to clothing extended to all his children. My father was a regular customer of the Esther Shop, a Washington institution dating from the 1930s that dressed children in the Eisenhower, Kennedy, and Johnson families and catered to diplomats by having a bilingual staff. According to my oldest sister, Carolyn, who was a child in the 1950s, most other downtown stores wouldn't allow Black customers inside, but the Esther Shop always welcomed my dad through the front door. He was an unusual father, in that he took us shopping and was quite capable of selecting our outfits on his own. Although my mother purchased most of my clothes—and we enjoyed many shopping trips as mother-daughter time—I too was taken to the Esther Shop so my father could choose outfits for me. I was too young to remember the shop's original location, but by the time I started Catholic school, its second storefront was inside the tony Mazza Gallerie in Northwest Washington. The shop's owners always greeted our family with warm intimacy, but I didn't play much of an active role in these purchasing sessions, being more of a mannequin than anything else as various garments were held up to my body for inspection.

Adding to my father's exterior sophistication was the fact that he could quote his favorite writer, William Shakespeare, with ease. The only times his diction betrayed his country upbringing was in his pronunciation of words such as *especially*, which he pronounced as *exspecially*, and *sink*, which he pronounced as *zink*. He enjoyed dining at all the posh spots in the city, which included Jean-Louis at the Watergate and Georgetown's 1789. So imagine my mother's shock and horror when she opened the refrigerator to find that my father had stored some squirrel meat he'd brought home from one of his La Plata visits. This was the food of his youth, just as kosher chickens were hers.

Although he was an able cook who enjoyed fixing Thanksgiving-style Sunday dinners year-round, my father was utterly undomestic in other ways. He didn't know how to assemble or repair equipment or cut the grass; nor did he care to learn. And he was not an outdoors person. The only nonhuman relationships I knew him to have were with our two family pets—a squat and mannish Scottish terrier named Zachary Taylor by my mother (because he looked like a little general), followed by Maggie, an inquisitive black Lab mix. My dad initially remained aloof to these furry creatures until they managed to wrap him around their little paws. Many a night my father greeted our Scottie at the door with a resounding "Zac! Zac my man," which set off a manic round of tail wagging. When the vet recommended that Zac be put to sleep after thirteen years, it was one of the rare times I saw my father cry. Still, the thought of my dad caring for cows is perplexing.

In contrast, I have a visceral and highly negative reaction to the idea of my father's labor being co-opted when he served time at Lorton. It is part of America's long history of exploiting the labor of Black people, especially Black men. For the last four hundred–plus years, since African people were abducted from their homes and forced into slavery, the United States has used their bodies to generate unprecedented wealth. This tradition continued after slavery in the guise of convict leasing (when Black men were arrested on trumped-up charges such as vagrancy and leased to mines and railroads), sharecropping, chain gangs, and other modern forms of under- and uncompensated labor. Some of America's most infamous prisons were Parchman Farm and Angola Farm (now known, respectively, as the Mississippi and Louisiana State Penitentiaries to disguise their histories as brutal plantations), where Black inmates were (and still are) forced to work for the benefit of the state and regional economies. The name Angola itself is telling—it was the homeland of the enslaved people who inhabited and worked the land in the nineteenth century.

12 *The Gambler*

Uncompensated or undercompensated labor is still the foundation of the US prison system, where incarcerated workers produce in excess of $2 billion annually in goods and commodities and $9 billion in services for the very facilities that imprison them.[3] The overwhelming majority of prison workers—cooks, groundskeepers, barbers, hospital workers, welders, carpenters, and others—report that they must comply with work assignments to avoid additional punishment. Some have even been called on to craft the deathbeds where lethal injections are administered. At Angola, for instance, "instead of purchasing a bed . . . the [Louisiana] Department of Corrections found it cheaper to direct the prisoners in the machine and welding shops to build it, with each part of the bed assembled separately." When the prisoners found out what they were building and refused to continue, they were locked in their cells.[4]

Most devastating was the realization that my family had been divided during my father's incarceration. I could now do more than intellectualize the time he served, because there was no one to change the subject or lie by omission. There was no one to cover up the fact that I had come into the world without his physical protection. And physical protection from the outside world, regardless of what happened inside our home, was one of the fundamental ways my father defined his role as patriarch of the Matthews family and as a Black father.

The Investigation

The arrests and indictments of Appellants were the culmination of a police investigation spanning a period of several months. During that time, officers of the Washington Metropolitan Police Department [Gambling Unit] four times sought and received judicial approval for limited telephone surveillance under the federal and local wiretap statutes. Appellants Odessa Marie Madre, John S. Matthews, Clyde N. Jones, and George Byers were convicted of operating a lottery know[n] as the numbers game, in violation of 22 D.C. Code, 1501 (1973). The [state and federal] statutes are essentially similar except that under the federal statute the business being done must average more than $2,000 a day.

PETITION FOR WRIT OF CERTIORARI, US COURT OF APPEALS FOR THE DISTRICT OF COLUMBIA CIRCUIT, AUGUST 30, 1976

Once I had confirmed the details of my dad's prison sentence, I wanted to learn about the circumstances of his arrest and the charges against him. I suppose this was the sleuth and the lawyer in me—although I no longer practice law, these habits are ingrained. I already knew from my mom that my father was represented by a former federal prosecutor who had established his own highly regarded law firm in Washington, DC. This was my starting place, and I sent him the following email:

14 *The Gambler*

> I hope this email finds you well. I am reaching out as the
> daughter of John Samuel Matthews, who passed away in 2013,
> and Lussia Matthews, who passed away in 2015. I have been
> seeking additional information on my father's incarceration
> in 1977 and any other related legal matters. I wondered if it
> may be possible for me to access any legal files that you have
> retained on this matter and if so what the process would be for
> doing so? I do not know what ethics rules allow in these in-
> stances. I appreciate your assistance and I am happy to discuss
> with someone at your firm if that is better. Thank you!

I received a speedy response, but it turned out I would have to
wait for the documents. Between the law firm's closure during the
COVID-19 pandemic and the fact that these old files were stored
off-site, the attorney would need a few months to review the files
to ensure that certain privileged work product materials were
withheld. Although I was eager to learn the truth, I was strangely
relieved to have more time to prepare myself for whatever facts
might come to light.

Approximately three months later, I was granted access to the
files. Because I lived in Nashville and could not safely travel due
to the pandemic, I sent my friend Nicole, a former attorney and
dogged researcher, to collect the files for me. She then used her
iPhone camera to send me those documents I wanted to access
immediately and mailed me the rest.

Through the various pleadings, correspondence, transcripts,
motions, and orders, I was able to assemble a detailed picture of
the investigation that unwittingly trapped my father, which I then
confirmed through my brother Johnny's firsthand recollections. I
was surprised that Johnny had never shared this information with
me, but then I realized that, given my complete ignorance, I hadn't
even known the right questions to ask. I also came to appreciate
that his knowledge was piecemeal, and some of what I discovered
gave him a broader understanding of what he had heard and seen
in real time.

The Investigation   15

The legal files confirmed the family whisperings that the FBI had a hand in my dad's conviction, but not in the way I expected. The FBI was interested in the narcotics trade, and Dad wasn't the original target. The feds had set their sights on two other people: Odessa Madre and Melvin Johnson.

Odessa Madre, the so-called queen of the underground, was a contemporary of my paternal grandmother, Nanny. Madre was born in 1907 in Cowtown, near Georgia and Florida Avenues NW. (The neighborhood's name came from the fact that cows, pigs, and sheep roamed free as late as the last decades of the nineteenth century.) Like my father, Madre was dark-skinned and therefore ostracized by the Black (often light-skinned) DC elite at Paul Lawrence Dunbar High School, the nation's first Black public high school. The city was renowned for its intraracial caste system, even as all Black people were fighting the white power structure. The paper-bag test was just one manifestation of this divide: anyone darker than a brown paper bag could not participate in certain sororities, fraternities, churches, or social events. In a *Washington Post* interview, Madre said, "There were only three Blacks at Dunbar back then—I mean Black like me. I had good diction, I knew the gestures, but they always made fun of me."[1]

In La Plata, my dad experienced the same colorism. On one of the many occasions I pressed him for details about his upbringing, he told me about being smitten with a girl from the Proctor family. "The Proctors were we-sorts, and they didn't want one of their daughters dating a dark-skinned boy," he said.

"What are we-sorts?" I asked, having never heard the term, which sounded like a word in a Dr. Seuss book.

"It's what we called the fair-skinned people," he replied. The term referred to a cluster of interrelated families in Charles and St. Mary's Counties in Maryland with a blended Native American, European, and Black heritage. "Their families liked to stay within themselves, among their own people," my father explained.

"So was we-sort kind of like 'we-sort of this, we-sort of that,' because they looked closer to white?" I asked, half-jokingly.[2]

16 *The Gambler*

My dad laughed. "Yes, you could say that!"

It occurs to me that one reason people like my father and Odessa gravitated to the underground world was that in those environments, color and pedigree didn't matter. What mattered was the ability to live by your wits, which is what gave you power and social standing.

Another similarity between Madre and my father was their skill at oratory. My father's ability to recite poetry—not only Shakespeare but also Coleridge and Kipling—was impressive. He had a record collection of Paul Robeson, Roscoe Lee Browne, Laurence Olivier, and John Gielgud reciting Shakespeare's soliloquies, which he listened to after the children had gone to bed and he wanted to unwind.

Paul Robeson was my dad's favorite thespian because he stayed true to his political convictions during the McCarthy-era Red Scare, while also possessing undeniable poise, integrity, and brilliance.[3] "Paul Robeson was many things, but he was an intelligent man first," my dad explained. "He rewrote the lyrics to the song 'Ol' Man River,'" he added, referring to the tune written for the musical *Show Boat.* He then launched into his best (albeit poor) impression of Robeson's bass vocals. Rather than singing of being "sick," "tired," and "skeered," Robeson refashioned the song into social commentary about the exploitation of Black labor and gave it a protest edge by introducing lyrics about "fightin'" and "showing grit," which landed the Black stevedore character in jail.[4]

My father and mother were so enamored with Mr. Robeson that they suggested him as the subject of my sixth-grade presentation on a notable cultural figure. I checked some books out of the library so I could show photos of Robeson, and on the day of the presentation I suited up in an oversized tuxedo with a red bow tie and matching cummerbund my mother rented from a bridal store. I attempted to deepen my voice and speak with as much of an oratorical flourish as my eleven-year-old self could muster, delivering Robeson's life story in the first person. I also played a recording of Robeson singing the spiritual "There Is a Balm in Gilead" for the unfamiliar ears of

The Investigation   17

my white private-school classmates. It was soul music in the truest sense, as he imbued pathos into the nineteenth-century lyrics:

> There is a balm in Gilead
> To make the wounded whole
> There is a balm in Gilead
> To heal the sin-sick soul
> Sometimes I feel discouraged
> And think my work's in vain
> But then the Holy Spirit
> Revives my soul again

My mind got stuck on *sin-sick* because it so perfectly mirrored the sense of weariness I absorbed from Robeson's vocals.

Like my father, Madre applied her intelligence to profit from the underground economy. Her business ventures were much more diversified than my father's street gambling, and she enjoyed considerable police protection during her heyday, which is extraordinary, considering the DC police force was mostly white Irishmen at the time. She knew some of these men from her old neighborhood, a predominantly German and Irish enclave. In addition to running street numbers, Madre was a bootlegger and a madam, and she was suspected of being involved in the city's narcotics trade. Even those who condemned her behavior expressed a grudging admiration for Madre. Retired police officer Miller Dixon said: "I had a lot of respect for Odessa. She was the only person I ever met who had just made the decision early on to be bad. She said, 'To hell with it,' and went on about her business."[5]

Odessa Madre was the "big get" in my father's case, according to the district court judge assigned to his trial. He noted that she had been "involved with the law since 1932" and had "done time at Alderson," the federal women's prison in West Virginia where singer Billie Holiday and Charles Manson acolyte Squeaky Fromme were also incarcerated. Feds hoped to uncover "the details of the scheme allegedly used by Odessa Madre and others then unknown

18   *The Gambler*

to smuggle illicit drugs into the United States and effect their sale and distribution thereafter."[6]

The other target of the original narcotics investigation, Melvin Johnson, is described in legal records as a longtime intimate and frequent companion of Madre's. Madre was known to be a lesbian, so this does not necessarily imply a sexual relationship. Johnson owned a men's clothing store called Chico's Men Shop and used pseudonyms, including Sam Macintosh, to conduct his business.

In 1973 the FBI utilized various tactics to surveil the pair. (It seems funny that *this* was the FBI's mission the year after the Watergate break-in.) The Bureau's suspicion was based in part on Madre's association with convicted narcotics traffickers Randolph "Catfish" Turner and Dennis Hopkins. Catfish had been arrested with $500,000 worth of cocaine in his car that same year. Consequently, the feds obtained pen registers (which provide only incoming and outgoing phone numbers, as opposed to wiretaps, which record full conversations) on two properties, including Odessa's home at 824 Aspen Street NW. After noting a suspicious number of incoming and outgoing calls, they obtained wiretaps on the same addresses. Under the 1968 Omnibus Crime and Safety Streets Act, this surveillance tool could be used to investigate a variety of criminal activities. Rather than narcotics trafficking, however, the taps uncovered brisk gambling activity.

I paged through one of the FBI transcripts of calls made in August 1974, which is largely a mundane, pages-long repetition of number combinations:

> Receiver: 51 25
> Caller: 51 25
> Receiver: 73 15
> Caller: 73 15
> Receiver: 3 95
> Caller: 3 95

But to me, it was as if I was eavesdropping on a conversation between my dad's friends Mr. Reds (named for his "red-bone" complexion

The Investigation 19

and narrow fox-like face) and Mr. Horace (rotund, unapproachable, and sedate). The coded language was almost as unintelligible as the messages my dad handled as a naval radioman during World War II.

> Caller: Horace had an "L" for 25 dollars.
> Receiver: Horace had an "L" for 25 dollars.
> Caller: Elaine nothing. Effie nothing. Reds nothing. WT nothing. X73 had an "L" for 650.
> Receiver: X73 L for 650.

Other individuals captured on the wiretap talk about their legal troubles:

> Receiver: They put me on probation.
> Caller: Yeh.
> Receiver: I got to go back on the 25 of October. You know find out how much probation they put me on.
> Caller: Uh ha.

I don't know if my father was part of this particular transcript, as there is no self-identifying language.

The FBI had discovered an altogether different brand of criminal activity than anticipated, but that didn't mean the investigation ended. Rather, the Metropolitan Police Department (MPD) took over from the feds. The numbers business was the progenitor of the contemporary betting game now played legally across the nation every day. But this style of street gambling, which had been popular in many segregated Black communities since at least the early twentieth century, was illegal. Enforcement actions against Black and brown numbers workers were common in many urban centers. Accounts of their arrests appeared in state and local newspapers, while other types of illegal gambling in white communities were downplayed or ignored. The MPD used the information gleaned in the FBI transcripts (in combination with other surveillance) to obtain a wiretap on another of Madre's properties on the second floor of 1900 16th Street, which became the focus of the gambling

20 *The Gambler*

investigation. In addition to installing a wiretap, undercover officers took photos of people going in and out during the day and collected bystander observations of the activity therein.

Subsequently, the MPD's Gambling Unit used the evidence gathered to apply for a search warrant of sixteen connected locations in the District of Columbia. "What we're talking about is a gambling operation which has tentacles that go all over the city and out to the racetracks and everything else. . . . Odessa Madre was really financing something—some of these operations—and . . . so were the others . . . and the sooner [the government] can get to the source . . . then you will stop the racket."[7]

On October 12, 1973, the squad arrested a group of twenty-six alleged gamblers, including my father. He had not been named in the warrant, but he was discovered hiding behind a refrigerator on the third floor of an apartment at 1326 U Street. Numbers slips totaling $600 in bets were found next to him. Shortly after his arrest, the MPD asked my father to provide handwriting exemplars and voiceprints. He was identified as the probable writer of two betting slips submitted for handwriting analysis, and his voice was captured on close to thirty phone calls. In all but four of the calls, he received the "service," meaning that he received information confirming the day's winning lottery numbers from Melvin Johnson or his son. The other calls were also gambling related. Because the $600 in bets linked to my father fell well short of the federal statute's threshold of $2,000 a day, prosecutors could only charge him under DC law. Eight months later, in June 1974, my dad was indicted for running an illegal lottery operation.

That December, his trial lawyer moved to suppress some of the evidence that implicated my father and one of his codefendants because the police hadn't notified them, as required by law, that their voices had been intercepted on a court-ordered wiretap. It turns out that my dad's name had been left off the government's list of the twenty-six individuals arrested, and his lawyer argued that the informal notice provided through interactions with a certain Officer Smith of the MPD was insufficient to compensate for this oversight. As I reviewed the hearing transcript, I could picture my dad suited up for court and acting the part of the perfectly composed witness because he knew the stakes were high:

Q: Do you recall that [according to Officer Smith's affidavit, after you were placed under arrest on October 12, 1973], that you . . . were informed inside the Gambling Squad office . . . that [your] oral conversations had been intercepted?

A: I recall reading [the affidavit] *this* morning [December 23, 1974], yes [emphasis added].

Q: Do you recall having seen Officer Smith . . . on October 12 of last year?

A: I saw him . . . at that time, but I didn't know who he was.

Q: Did you have a conversation with Officer Smith on that date?

A: Officer Smith didn't process me, because I think he led several raids that day.

Q: On October 25 of 1973, you and other defendants in this case went and had voiceprints made? Do you recall that?

A: Yes.

Q: Do you recall having a conversation with Officer Smith on that day?

A: If I saw Officer Smith on that day, I don't recall, because Officer Smith is Black and there was a white fellow who conducted the voiceprints.

Q: Did Officer Smith on that date tell you that some of your conversations had been intercepted.

A: No, sir. May I say this, . . . prior to—the only time that I met Officer Smith to be informed as to who he was, it was the day [October 19, 1973] where we all went to Court.

Despite the best efforts of my father and his attorney, the motion to suppress was denied, and my dad was ultimately convicted and sentenced in January 1975 to six to eighteen months in prison.

At this point, my father hired a new lawyer—the one I had contacted to obtain his files—to make the novel legal arguments required to appeal his conviction based on the illegality of the wiretap.

22 *The Gambler*

My father remained free on bond as his appeal made its way through the federal court system. In January 1977 his final possible appeal to the US Supreme Court was denied. In a last-ditch effort to keep him out of prison, my father's attorney filed a motion to reduce his sentence to probation, citing my father's familial responsibilities, the grief and anxiety his children were experiencing in the aftermath of the death of my father's common-law wife, Judy, from brain cancer (the birth mother of my half-sister Megan), and the intellectual promise his children showed:

> The family depends more so than ever on Mr. Matthews. He is responsible for the support of seven unusual and extremely able children in various stages of their education. He is responsible for the emotional stability of these children at a time when the family group has endured an extraordinary degree of pressure and severe loss. . . . As the presentence report in this case indicates, the Matthews family is an unusual family. Under Mr. Matthews [sic] guidance, his children have achieved great social and educational success. (His oldest son [Michael] was offered an appointment to the Naval Academy.) We do not believe the community would be served in any respect if Mr. Matthews were removed from his position as family head and incarcerated as a penalty for his conviction for operating a lottery. Given the degree of responsibility and commitment to a life of accomplishment and value that he has repeatedly demonstrated, Mr. Matthews is a fit and able subject for probationary guidance and counseling. . . . Indeed, the guidance and therapy that are available through the Probation Office would benefit the entire family at a time when their needs are considerable.[8]

After reading this motion, I had to pause for a minute to absorb the unintended ambiguity of the phrase "He is responsible for the emotional stability of these children." Although my father provided material support and was a stalwart presence in the lives of his children, he was also a major source of our mental turmoil and anxiety. Many of us were gifted, performed well in school, and appeared poised to the outside world, but we also manifested both outward and inward signs of abuse. Some of us were so terrified that we were *too* well behaved; others were belligerent, angry, and rebellious. Although we lacked the knowledge to label it at the time, post-traumatic stress disorder (PTSD), adverse childhood experiences (ACEs), and childhood anxiety disorders profoundly marked and distorted our early years and then bled into our adulthoods.

Despite the heartfelt motion, no sentence reduction was granted. My father would serve eight months in Lorton. The original targets of the investigation received harsher sentences: Odessa Madre got one to three years, and Melvin Johnson was sentenced to twenty months to five years.

The Lottery

My father was what was known as a numbers man. Most people in the working-class Black communities of Washington, DC (and sometimes beyond), were acquainted with this daily game of chance. If you weren't related to someone or didn't know someone who worked in the numbers, you at least knew people who played them.

Running a street lottery was a crime, and the networks of people who operated these complex gambling enterprises were breaking the law, especially if the mob was involved. But did this crime warrant the level of effort the feds and then the DC police put into building a case against my father and his colleagues? This is a question I struggle to answer. DC was not Chicago or New York or New Jersey, where the mob reigned supreme. Operating a numbers game was not an inherently violent offense. Add to that the hypocrisy of national developments surrounding gambling: in 1976, the year before I was born, a presidential commission made recommendations about how to address illegal gambling; at the same time, several state governments were moving to legalize their own lottery schemes to avoid tax increases.

For decades prior to the establishment of officially sanctioned lotteries, police departments in major cities aggressively targeted numbers operations. Notably, when Richard Nixon accepted the nomination for president in 1968, he railed against numbers racketeers and pledged to pursue them alongside organized crime and peddlers of filth and narcotics in an effort to save the urban poor

The Lottery   25

and the country's children from being victimized. Caught up in these enforcement efforts were people like my father—mostly men, but also some women—for whom the street lottery supplied a good livelihood (and tax-free earnings), as well as helped to support and capitalize institutions in communities where traditional financing wasn't always available.

To understand my father's decision to participate in the numbers, it is important to understand the significance of this betting scheme in Black communities during the heyday of segregation and in its aftermath. The street lottery was a vital part of the extralegal economy that allowed those largely excluded from the mainstream economy to support themselves. Bettors could place daily, inexpensive wagers on three-digit number combinations; a related betting game called policy was popular among Chicagoans. Harlem Renaissance poet Claude McKay described the numbers as "an open, simple and inexpensive game of chance . . . a people's game, a community pastime in which old and young, literate and illiterate, the neediest folk and the well-to-do all participate."[1]

The winning numbers were based on horse races or other verifiable published sources. The bets were small, so it was a relatively low-risk gamble, and the standard tax-free payoff was 600 to 1. However, when a number was extremely popular, the payoff would be cut so as not to wipe out the numbers "bank." The most successful operations were complex affairs with many moving parts. Like all corporate structures, there was a hierarchy that allowed the operation to run smoothly. At the bottom were the numbers writers—the basic street-level workers who wrote and collected the bets and earned commissions on these transactions. Some operations also employed runners to deliver the betting slips and the money. At the top were the bankers, also called backers, who ensured that winners were paid off. They worked with numerous runners and writers. Large bankers might support smaller bankers, charging interest to backstop any big payoffs the smaller bankers couldn't handle themselves. Also essential to the operation was the service office—a contact at the racetrack charged with monitoring the races. The service office relayed each winning digit from the races in real time to prevent bettors from "past posting," or scrambling to play numbers that had already been called.

My father was a prominent numbers banker and bookie in DC. He had a series of writers and runners who took and carried bets for him in all four quadrants of DC, although a lot of his business was in upper northwest DC along Georgia Avenue, which had a significant Black population. He was not the biggest banker in the business, however. As Johnny recalled, when the numbers hit big, my father worked with larger bankers to make sure he could pay both his hits and commissions without depleting his bank. This collaboration was called laying off a bet. Think of my father as a regional bank with great personal service that was backed up by a multinational bank like Bank of America. When the larger bankers covered his hits, they charged him 25 cents on the dollar and allowed him to pay them back in installments or in full. My father also loaned money to individuals and charged interest. In the 1960s he carried a pistol for protection, according to my brother; by the 1970s, his word and his reputation meant that he no longer needed the gun.

Numbers operators like my father were, in effect, the dream makers of the people who placed bets with them. This is not merely because of the so-called dream books some bettors used to translate their reveries and nighttime visions into sets of three-digit numbers. It is because the men and women who placed bets looked up to and wanted to be like these numbers operators, who were frequently philanthropic and shared their winnings by making gifts to schools, civil rights organizations, sports teams, and churches in their communities. When John Lewis and the other brave young Freedom Riders desperately needed cash to buy bus tickets and food to continue their dangerous journey from Nashville to Birmingham, they turned to a Nashville numbers runner. "So here, at ten o'clock at night . . . we said, 'Who would have money on a Sunday night?' So we went to the numbers man in Nashville— a numbers man always has cash. So he took [our unendorsed check]."[2]

My father's philanthropy stayed close to home. He helped people pay rent and tuition and buy clothes, and he gave generously to his church, St. Augustine's. Although he was driven to provide the best of everything for his large family, if he had it to give, he would not turn his back on those in desperate straits. I think this was because he knew what it was to want, to not have life's basic necessities.

There were those in the Black community who frowned on the numbers racket because they thought it sullied the reputations of Black people as a group. This was the argument of so-called respectability politics—that we all had to be morally upright as defined by mainstream white society. Some of this crowd also believed that the numbers game was exploitative because it fed gambling addictions, especially among the lower-income folks who bet frequently. To these people, the numbers men and women were not dream makers but parasites.

But it was undeniable that, for a time, the numbers provided a means of uplift. My father essentially presided over his own Black version of the Rat Pack, as he and his colleagues outfitted themselves in designer suits and shoes. He was able to buy both his own house and a house for his mother in the neighborhood where he operated his business. These were the first homes owned by anyone in his family, and given the entrenched disparities in Black home ownership and generational wealth and the lack of mortgages and other loans accessible to Black people, this was a tremendous accomplishment.[3] It is a story that echoes the experience of Secretary of State Colin Powell, who credits numbers winnings for enabling his family to purchase their first home at a time when mortgages were virtually impossible to come by for Black people.

Thus, the numbers game reflected the American values of entrepreneurialism and pluck, which were encouraged and admired in white men but not in Black men. Like his contemporary Malcolm X (who also worked in the numbers for a time), my father's secret boyhood dream was to become a lawyer. Given his quick wit, facility with the written word, and penchant for the dramatic, he would have made a splendid trial lawyer. Unfortunately, even sharing such an ambition with anyone would have been suicide at the time. Les Payne could have been describing my father when he wrote in his biography of Malcolm X, "It was not so much a doorman's job or a shoeshine stand that his buddies saw in Malcolm's future but rather the prison tier, and beyond that, most likely, they agreed, an early grave. With few lucky exceptions, that's just the way American life in the 1940s was engineered for bold, highly intelligent, fast-tick Negro men without a support system—even those who wanted to become lawyers."[4]

Some numbers operators were so brilliant that even the police expressed a grudging admiration for their entrepreneurial skill. As Sergeant Bernard Emmert of the DC gambling squad stated, "I have a lot of respect for them. If a lot of those guys put their resourcefulness into something legitimate, there's no telling what they could achieve."[5] The problem was that many of those who turned to the numbers did so because their choices were limited, and they had no clear path to a legitimate and fulfilling means of making a living. They couldn't change the system, but they could opt out of it.

Trouble Man

I never asked my father how his numbers career began, but given the social and cultural context of his youth, it's no mystery. I believe a combination of factors was at work. First, a survival mechanism for many Black Americans was learning the art of the hustle. It was simply what they did to make ends meet when their meager wages didn't support them and their families. If it bucked the "system" and offended the "man" in some way, so be it. My paternal grandmother, for instance, cleaned white people's houses by day, but she also made extra money as a bootlegger. Second, my father may have been inspired by race men and women like Paul Robeson, who would not settle for second-class citizenship. And finally, the numbers bore a certain nexus to his naval career as a code man.

Trying to place myself in my father's world—or "walk a mile in his shoes," as he liked to say—brings to mind Octavia Butler's *Kindred*. Each time the novel's protagonist, Dana, is transported between the 1970s and the antebellum Maryland of her Black and white ancestors, she suffers irrevocable psychological and physical harm. This is the bane of trading ignorance to learn history.

Although I am not traveling back as far as Dana, my father was fifty-three at the time of my birth—an age difference more typical of a grandparent and grandchild. He was a member of the Greatest Generation, while I was at the tail end of Generation X. Between his birth and mine, there were many legislative advances and political victories in the name of civil rights and human rights, but these decades also witnessed incredible carnage and domestic terrorism.

Like the protagonist in *Kindred*, my father's story starts in Maryland. He grew up in the southern part of the state, on the Western Shore of the Chesapeake Bay. His hometown of La Plata, now the seat of Charles County, is located thirty miles southeast of Washington, DC. It was incorporated as a railroad town after the Pennsylvania Railroad came through the area. Although slavery in the Deep South states of Mississippi, Louisiana, and Georgia is most often featured cinematically, the Chesapeake had its own distinct and deep-seated tradition of that peculiar institution, based on tobacco farming.

I can trace my father's ancestors in Maryland back to the 1830s, thanks to the inclusion of Black people in the 1870 census for the first time, but like so many other African Americans, I lose the thread at this point. Those of us with enslaved ancestors learn to be critical readers rather than textualists because the most essential parts of our stories are often not recorded in writing.

From the 1930 census, I can tell that members of my dad's family—with names such as Basil, Victoria, Isabelle, and Elizabeth—were laborers and domestics. Although there could be many reasons, including mimicry of white Victorian cultural norms, I like to think my great-grandmother named all her daughters after queens as a way to assert that, someday, we as a people could achieve more.

My father's birth in 1924 placed him within three generations of slavery in his family. According to family lore, one of my father's great-grandfathers ran away from a Maryland plantation to join the Union army, and his grandfather's white cousins were related to one of the signatories of the Declaration of Independence. Things hadn't changed all that much for rural Black people in the decades since slavery's abolition. Like so many others, my father lived under a system of racial apartheid in which Black people were kept impoverished and denied the full rights of citizenship. Even learning to read was considered a revolutionary act.

My father was raised by his maternal grandparents, Seymour and Lizzie Simms. His mother, whom we grandchildren called Nanny, was an unwed seventeen-year-old at the time of his birth—just as her mother had been prior to her long-term marriage to Nanny's father.[1] After the midwife delivered John Samuel Simms (the name on my father's birth record), Nanny moved to the nation's capital to work as a domestic so that she could send her wages home to the family. She also may have left to escape her mother's wrath, as it turns out that my father was not Nanny's first child; she had a stillborn baby before him. John Samuel would remain her only living child.

According to the 1930 census, Seymour and Lizzie Simms were living with four of their children, their five-year-old grandson (my father), and three other children under the age of ten, who were likely cousins or neighbors. As my father once explained to me, you might be poor, but you didn't turn away someone who needed a home. Seymour, age fifty-six, was listed as a farm laborer, while fifty-two-year-old Lizzie was employed as a family cook.

My father was too young to remember the deadly tornado that ripped through his hometown in 1926, but he did recall the 1933 lynching of a twenty-three-year-old Black man named George Armwood in Princess Anne, on the opposite shore of the Chesapeake Bay. The Eastern Shore of Maryland, known simply as the Shore, had long been isolated from the remainder of the state and thus developed a distinct culture that had more in common with Virginia and Delaware than with Baltimore, DC, or Philadelphia.[2]

George Armwood was just one of the nearly sixty-five hundred (overwhelmingly Black) people lynched in the United States between 1877 and 1950. The Eastern Shore had conducted its fair share of lynchings since before the Civil War, including a gruesome quadruple execution that took place in Princess Anne in 1869.[3]

Prior to his lynching, Armwood's living conditions were no better than slavery. After he finished fifth grade, his mother, out of economic necessity, had turned him over to a white man, Mr. Richardson, to work as a laborer. When George was accused of robbing

32   *The Gambler*

and assaulting an eighty-two-year-old white woman, he became the latest victim of lynching. The young man was dragged from his jail cell and fed to a mob of around two thousand people. He was stabbed and mutilated, hung from a tree, and burned. The leaders of the mob were never punished.[4] My father never mentioned this harrowing event to me, and neither my mother nor my siblings had ever heard him talk about it either. It is a hallmark of deep generational trauma to bury memories of such extreme acts of genocide and domestic terror.[5]

I happened to read an account of the lynching in 2004, when I was researching antilynching activism in my last year of law school. I called my father to see what he could share, if anything, about the incident. I knew he was only nine years old at the time of this savage act (a headline called it a "Roman Holiday"). I also knew he had started to show signs of dementia, but sometimes people suffering from memory loss and disorientation can recall the past with startling clarity. "Yes, I *do* remember that," he said, his voice unusually tender. "The man's name was George Armwood. I remember the older folks talking. I remember they were scared."

From the distance of seven decades, the memory of George Armwood was seared into his soul. In some ways, my father's vivid recall of this early childhood incident is representative of the experience of many African American children exposed to this gruesome and uniquely American form of violence. It was common for youngsters to eavesdrop on the hushed conversations of grown folks. The stories they overheard were often such vivid cautionary tales that later, as adults, their retellings contained many accurate details.[6]

Dad's recollection of the lynching made me reflect on previous interactions, such as his insistence that I not travel to the Eastern Shore at night to visit a white coworker who lived there. I went anyway, and not surprisingly, my Black friend and I were flagged down on the way home by a police officer, on the pretext that my friend was driving drunk. We counted our lucky stars when my friend passed her sobriety test and the officer grudgingly let us go. Well into the twenty-first century, Sherrilyn Ifill, former president

Trouble Man 33

and director-counsel of the NAACP Legal Defense Fund, was routinely warned by Black Marylanders about crossing the Bay Bridge as she traveled the state, working with clients. As she states, "a town's reputation as racially violent often lives on in the lore shared among" Black communities.[7]

I was also reminded of a sordid story my father had told me about his youth. When he was around ten years old, he worked for a white bootlegger who had two teenage daughters. In addition to the indignity of having to sing minstrel songs for this white man, my father was sexually molested by the daughters. I can imagine how terrified he must have been to know that anything these older girls did to him, even by force, would mean certain death for him if they were caught.

In his short life, he had already faced racial terrorism and natural disaster. Then, at age fourteen, my father lost his guardian angel and grandfather Seymour. Seymour was a gentle man whose health had long been compromised by rheumatic fever. While Seymour was alive, he had provided security and stability for his young grandson, but without him, my father's world suddenly became unbearable. His grandmother was both physically and verbally abusive to him, as were his twin uncles Joe and Edward. When Grandma Lizzie remarried, her new husband complained about the expense of feeding my father, who ate too much. To rectify the situation, she kicked John Samuel out of her house.

Perhaps another family member in La Plata took him in for a time (he had lots of aunts and uncles), or perhaps Lizzie allowed him to return, because my father graduated from La Plata's segregated Bel Alton High School in 1941. He was among the school's first group of graduates. He spoke admiringly of his teachers as community role models who instilled racial pride in their students. This was part of the strange blessing of segregation—the teachers felt a sense of responsibility to their students, beyond teaching classroom lessons. Decades later, my dad could still proudly recite the poetry he had learned as a schoolboy. One of his favorites was Rudyard Kipling's "If," both ironic and prophetic:

> If you can make one heap of all your winnings
> And risk it on one turn of pitch-and-toss,
> And lose, and start again at your beginnings
> And never breathe a word about your loss
> Yours is the Earth and everything that's in it,
> And—which is more—you'll be a Man, my son!

When he reached manhood, my father was living with his mother in Washington, DC, on 13th and V Streets, the heart of the U Street corridor where he would later run his numbers business. He was part of a new wave of low-income or working-class migrants to the city from the South. This neighborhood in Northwest DC earned the nickname Black Broadway because it was an enclave of possibility and Black self-expression within the segregated city. This area is the home of Howard University, the crown jewel of the historically Black college and university (HBCU) system and a longtime hub of Black intellectualism.

U Street was also an artistic center, filled with theaters that "featured films, floor shows, musicals, and vaudeville" and where the likes of Duke Ellington, Louis Armstrong, Billie Holiday, Ella Fitzgerald, and Cab Calloway performed and hung out unmolested by white Washingtonians.[8] Because of the strict racial segregation that prohibited Black residents from patronizing downtown hotels, restaurants, and businesses, Black Broadway attempted to create everything it needed to be self-sustaining. As a *Washingtonian* article titled "The Forgotten History of U Street" reveals, Black people made a world for themselves within the confines of an apartheid system: "Everybody knew everybody," said Richard Lee, whose parents opened Lee's Flower Shop at 928 U Street in 1945. "We didn't miss going downtown. We didn't give a shit. I mean, excuse my language, but they wanted to have all that stuff to themselves, fine—we had all this stuff to ourselves."[9] Later, the U Street area would become a base for the civil rights organizing of Martin Luther King Jr. and John Lewis, and it was the site of one of the many riots in the aftermath of King's death.

Despite civil service test scores that qualified him for a better position, the Government Printing Office (GPO) offered my father the most menial job: pressman's helper. This was the order of the day in 1940s Washington. For a brief time after the Civil War, some Black residents were granted the rights of citizenship. The Civil Rights Amendments (the Thirteenth, Fourteenth, and Fifteenth Amendments to the US Constitution) enfranchised Black men and gave them the right to serve on juries. DC also passed ordinances that prohibited theaters, pubs, hotels, and other public establishments from discriminating against Black patrons. However, these changes did not last long. Although a cadre of Black social elites would exercise a degree of privilege that was not possible in the South, Jim Crow segregation still characterized a number of DC's institutions and thereby foreclosed opportunities. And for the impoverished Black refugees from the South who settled in DC in record numbers, their existence was often hand to mouth.

The federal government remained one of the last bastions of social mobility and wealth for Black Washingtonians, until President Woodrow Wilson resegregated the federal workforce. Whites and Blacks were relegated to separate facilities, Black supervisors were dismissed, and the best-paying jobs and promotions were reserved for white employees.

In October 1943, after a year of employment at the GPO, my nineteen-year-old father was inducted into the US Navy. When President Franklin Roosevelt first reinstated the peacetime draft in the midst of growing Nazi aggression, he did not mince words about where the burden should fall: "I say that democracy is your cause, the cause of the youth." Left unsaid was how this burden fell even more heavily on young Black men, who were also forced to battle for democracy on the home front.

While the armed forces reserved mostly unskilled roles for Black servicemen, my father was a radioman. His high scores on the general classification test plus growing pressure on the US Navy to better accommodate Black seamen resulted in him spending nineteen weeks at the Naval Training School in Great Lakes,

36   *The Gambler*

Illinois, learning the various skills he would need to receive radio signals and process shipboard telecommunications.[10] Radioman is a naval classification that did not exist until three years prior to my father's birth, so they came of age together. In a World War II training film, radiomen are lauded as "vital to the security of the Navy, vital to the maintenance of its communications, and vital to its effectiveness as a formidable striking power that will bring [the Allied powers] to final victory." Having "earned the respect of their officers and their shipmates, they are . . . the nerves of the Navy." All the men featured in this film as they type, practice code, and repair equipment are white.

My father was stationed in the Pacific. The most essential part of his job was encrypting and decrypting messages using Morse code. Even decades after his service, he would playfully mimic the sounds of the dots and dashes of this complex language, which has its own percussive charm. Like some of the poetry he learned at school, he never forgot Morse code.

My father mostly avoided discussing the painful memories of World War II, but he did share what it meant to be a Black serviceman prior to President Harry Truman's 1948 executive order desegregating the military. During radio training, he wasn't allowed to enter the areas where the white WAVES (Women Accepted for Voluntary Emergency Service) worked. A well-meaning white officer urged my father to come directly to him if any of his white peers tried to start an altercation; otherwise, the blame would inevitably fall on my dad. He went for months without a haircut on the ship because none of the white seamen would deign to cut a Black man's hair. And then there was his one wartime souvenir: a nearly three-foot-long samurai sword kept behind the padlocked door leading to the attic. What remained unsaid was that this war trophy had been part of a life-and-death struggle with a Japanese soldier. He would eventually tell me that he'd seen a psychiatrist after the war to work through the trauma of holding a dying man in his arms, his abdomen opened wide and deep enough to expose his intestines.

My father was in Tokyo Bay when General Douglas MacArthur accepted the Japanese surrender on the USS *Missouri*. He spoke with empathy about the desperate Japanese civilians scavenging for sustenance, yet he could never rid himself of the vocabulary of combat, always referring to his wartime enemy as "Japs." He also claimed to have a Japanese girlfriend by the name of Yukiko Suzuki, who begged him not to leave her behind. (Sometimes, when my imagination was particularly fertile, I'd fantasize about having an octogenarian half-Japanese sibling.) After two years, seven months, and thirteen days in the navy, my dad was honorably discharged and headed back to the United States. His discharge papers note his desire for additional business training after the war.

Ostensibly, anyone who served a minimum of ninety days and had not been dishonorably discharged was entitled to receive, under the GI Bill signed into law by FDR, living expenses and a tuition waiver to attend an institution of higher education. But the chair of the House Veterans Committee was the rabidly racist John Rankin of Mississippi. He drafted the GI Bill to ensure that the approximately 1.2 million Black veterans would have to seek funds from their local veterans administrations, which would discriminate against them by either denying benefits outright or steering them away from higher education toward technical and vocational programs. Although HBCUs were open to Black veterans, these institutions could not absorb the same number of students accepted by other better-funded universities and colleges. As a result, the GI Bill "actually widened educational and economic gaps between [Black and] white Americans."[11]

Home ownership was also denied to Black veterans. The low-interest mortgages and loans guaranteed by the Veterans Administration were largely unavailable to them.[12] This only exacerbated the housing segregation resulting from the practice of redlining, which essentially branded all Black neighborhoods as too high-risk for financial institutions to invest in. Thus, the GI Bill was another means by which America transferred wealth to white communities and away from Black communities, perpetuating the wealth disparities that persist between the races to this day.

My father was discharged from the military with a total discharge pay of $336.37, a few victory ribbons, and not much more.

38 *The Gambler*

There was no higher education, no business course, and no home ownership to help catapult him into the ranks of the middle class. Given his limited options, my father took a roofing job and went back to work at the GPO, at least until 1950.[13] The hot tar used in roofing disfigured his forearms, leaving painful scars that drew my little-girl eyes every time he rolled up his shirtsleeves. Two decades later, I no longer registered the scars as distinct from his facial features or his mustache. But seeing the Arlington Courthouse skyline must have elicited a phantom pain. "I did that one [roof] right there," he said wistfully, pointing out the passenger window as we passed one of the nondescript squat brick buildings, some of which were now cheap motels.

There is a balm in Gilead
To make the wounded whole
There is a balm in Gilead
To heal the sin-sick soul.

Part 2
THE GRADUATE

The Early Years

I'm fascinated by the interplay of genealogical inheritance and coincidence. I've watched several episodes of the PBS series *Finding Your Roots* hosted by Henry Louis Gates Jr., as well as the TLC equivalent *Who Do You Think You Are?* The inexplicable parallels between the celebrity guests and the lives of those who preceded them never fail to astonish me. For instance, one episode of *Who Do You Think You Are?* featured actress Liv Tyler and her father Steven Tyler, of Aerosmith fame. Although Steven Tyler is best known as the lead singer of power rock ballads like "Dream On," he started his musical career as a drummer. However, it was only well into his sixth decade that Tyler discovered he was the descendant of two generations of Black military drummers—his four-times great-grandfather, who was present at the Battle of Plattsburg during the War of 1812, and his three-times great-grandfather Robert, a Union army drummer at Antietam and Gettysburg during the Civil War.

What really compelled Steven Tyler to become a drummer? Was it fated by something embedded in his subconscious, or was it all just wondrous serendipity? What proclivities do our forebears, our genes, and our unique family histories (even if unknown) imprint on us? Is it synaptic? Is it passed on in the dreams we forget? Do our fathers (and our mothers) whisper secrets to us while we slumber? How, we ask ourselves, do we end up here? How do we become the people we are? What compels us to choose how we spend our days? Why are we motivated to do the things we do?

42   *The Graduate*

As a young law student, I worked with an inmate on Alabama's death row, and as I gradually built a rapport with my client, it dawned on me that he was my father's "here but for the grace of God" incarnation. Almost twenty years later, this connection is even more apparent. During my time in Alabama, I started to comprehend for the first time how structural, systemic, and institutional racism often determines a person's opportunities (or lack thereof), responses, and choices, leaving me with the following questions: When a person commits a deplorable act, how much weight is assigned to the individual versus the culture? Where does that leave those of us who are directly impacted by the act in question? How is this calculus affected when the offender is a loved one?

To answer these questions in connection with my father meant starting at the beginning—my beginning—and reinterpreting my relationships with my father and my mother through this new lens, as well as exploring what held them together as a couple for so long.

My earliest memories are of the house on Evarts Street NE where I spent the first years of my life. It was bursting at the seams with kids: me, my four teenage brothers from my father's second marriage to Cora, and my sister Megan from his common-law marriage to Judy. With my parents, that added up to eight people in a fourteen hundred–square foot house. I slept in a crib in my parents' room for the three years we lived there, which explains why I was old enough to yell at my father to stop his "damn whoring" (I meant "snoring") in the middle of the night. (It seems that in addition to acquiring the habit of swearing, I had an unfortunate speech impediment.) My rotating cast of brothers stayed in the attic, and my sister, the only other girl, had a room to herself across the hall from my parents' first-floor master bedroom.

My memories of this house are few, but two stand out. It was 1980 or 1981, and I was three or four years old. I remember my mother sitting on the couch in the living room while my father stood menacingly over her. His emotion was easy to read, even if I couldn't understand the words—he spoke loudly, with rage-filled inflections. I cowered on the floor next to the couch. Suddenly, he thrust out his hand, which must have been holding a glass or bottle of beer. I can still see the splash of golden-colored liquid splatter on the wall directly behind my mom and her long hair fan out in wet glistening threads plastered to it. She is forever preserved in my mind as Our Lady of the Perpetual Fear, resembling one of those somber figures in the stained-glass windows I observed while attending mass at St. Augustine's.

The other memory might have been a dream, or possibly a consequence of my later consumption of too many gothic novels about children who lived in attics. But to this day, I am convinced there was a secret corridor in the attic of that house. I can see it so vividly— me trudging up the cramped stairs and then tucking myself into a small cubbyhole that ascended to an expansive white space with billowy curtains and comfortable window seats that only I seemed to know about. But every time I concentrated too hard on unraveling the secrets of this magical place, it slipped from my grasp. Once I asked Megan about this secret space—specifically, how it could fit into our tiny house. But my sister, whose boundless imagination created fantastical plays involving our dolls, just stared at me quizzically. From that point on, I treated my knowledge of the secret attic gently, keeping it safe and taking it out only when I needed it.

When I was four years old we moved to my deceased grandmother's house in Northwest Washington—the house my mother grew up in. This house had an attic too, but not one I wanted to spend any time in. It was behind a padlocked door, and it was musty and hot, with green walls.

At that time, I wondered, did all daddies hit mommies? All I knew was that when my daddy came home angry, the rest of us suffered. I didn't know what made him so mad, but he took it out on my mom. There was always name-calling within the four walls of our house: shitass, dummy, bitch. Daddy called my mother "dumb bitch" when he got worked up, right before he started pounding and punching. She would plead and cry for him to stop, and then I would cry too. There was no buildup to his rage when he came home after a bad day. It was like a big wave crashing on the beach,

44　*The Graduate*

with me feeling small and powerless and unable to grab anything to keep myself afloat. I yearned for my secret attic to hide in during these moments, but it had vanished for good. My mom, my sister, my brothers, and I bore the marks of those outbursts long afterward, but my daddy acted like he had forgotten all about it the next day. Was that possible? He never looked ashamed—not even when he had grabbed my mom by the throat or the arm or pushed her. And he never apologized. (When Megan and I fought, I would slip little notes under her door about "wanting to be sisters again," even though our arguments were mostly her fault, and then we would make up.) It was impossible for me to forget how my daddy had acted, but I couldn't stop talking to him every time he got mad, because then I would never talk to him again.

One day, when they were fighting in their bedroom, I tried to intervene but only succeeded in making my mom mad at me. It sounded like she was in trouble—I heard her howl—and the wall was vibrating. I pushed on the closed bedroom door, but it was hard to open; I finally got it to budge by putting all my weight against it. Once I was inside, my mom turned to me with tears in her eyes, her face red and puffy, and yelped, "Why would you hit me in my back?" I didn't know she had been leaning against the door. I hung my head and ran away, ashamed. I didn't understand why she blamed me when Daddy was the one screaming at her.

Even so, I really loved my daddy. He could be pretty funny and was a good storyteller. He gave me two of my favorite nicknames: the Queen and Onika. I used to giggle wildly when he flipped his eyelids inside out, turned his hands into claws, and chased me around the room. He sang me a Negro spiritual he had been taught as a child. He didn't have the best voice, but he put a lot of feeling into it. The song mentioned all the things God's children (which Daddy pronounced *chil'run*) had when they got up to heaven—a robe, shoes, a harp. He stuck his mustached lip out a little and strutted around while he performed it. My favorite part of the song was:

Heav'n, Heav'n
Ev'rybody talkin' 'bout Heav'n ain't goin' there

Heav'n, Heav'n
Goin' to shout all over God's Heaven

He took in a breath for each "Heaven." For the second line, he only inhaled before "Ev'rybody"; the other words just tumbled out. He taught me that the right way to sing the word *heaven* in this song was to swallow the second syllable. This was my playful daddy.

Daddy always checked on me at night to make sure I was actually sleeping and not trying to read by my nightlight. I liked to scooch down to the bottom of my four-poster bed so I could see the pages better. My readers at school were full of stories and quizzes you had to answer before moving on to the next chapter and then advance to the next level reader. I was trying to beat one of my classmates, Linda, and finish more pages so that I could take the classroom quizzes first. On those nights, Daddy would just lift me up and tuck me back into bed. He liked to read in bed late at night too; he had lots of magazines and books at his bedside.

Another thing about Daddy was that he was very patient and tender when removing the splinters I got from going sockless on our hardwood floors. He used a needle that he cleaned first with wintergreen alcohol or witch hazel and a cotton ball. Sometimes it hurt, and when I winced, he would say "sorry" and talk to me calmly. He could get the splinter out no matter how deep it went.

He didn't kiss me all the time or tell me he loved me, like my mom did. But when I was sick, he would come into my bedroom and put his hand on my forehead. He would ask me how I felt and whether I was in pain. He'd bring me anything I wanted to eat or drink and set it up on a little side table for me to use while I watched TV in bed. If I needed to blow my nose, he gave me his handkerchief. He was a good daddy then. I think he loved me.

My father didn't drive. Either he hitched rides with my mom or his Cadillac- and Lincoln Town Car–driving friends—their shiny cars smelled like a combination of sweet, pungent cigars and pine air freshener—or he walked. My mother's explanation was that he had soured on driving after the war and simply chose not to. For

46   *The Graduate*

someone who got so irate when people or events ran late, it was surprising that he placed his fate in the hands of others, but then again, maybe he knew road rage would get him in trouble.

Our cars weren't flashy like the ones my dad's friends drove. We had a blue Omega—or Homega, as I called it. My mom used to take me driving in the Homega when I couldn't sleep as an infant. One time, she put my purple pillow on the roof of the car, forgot about it, and drove off. We found the pillow in a ditch by the house. I stopped my mewling upon its recovery, but I would shed more tears when the Homega was put out to pasture and replaced with a white Cutlass Sierra. I always got easily attached to things and people and found myself heartbroken by even the smallest losses.

In the car, my mother was faithful to the radio stations that played oldies classics—dreamy Philadelphia soul and Motown artists such as Teddy Pendergrass, the Supremes, the Four Tops, the Temptations, and Marvin Gaye, especially when he was dueting with Tammi Terrell or Kim Weston. Mom didn't sing along because of her tone deafness, but I could tell by the way she nodded her head that this music was her favorite. I loved it too.

So when Marvin Gaye died in 1984 and Diana Ross recorded the ballad "Missing You," mourning her friend, my mother wanted me to learn the vocals. I had already been playing classical violin for three years and had just started to sing informally. My mom encouraged this newfound talent when my music teacher told her I had near-perfect pitch. Together, we wandered the aisles of Dale's Music, where we sometimes took my violin for retuning because it was too hard for my small hands to turn the pegs myself. We found the sheet music for the song—a glossy white booklet with Marvin's smiling, bearded face on the cover. As we left the store, I asked, "Mom, how did Marvin Gaye die?"

My mother paused, looked at me with unvarnished hurt in her eyes, and said, "Marvin was hurt by his father."

"His father did that to him?"

"His father had a bad temper and couldn't control himself," she explained. Then she said, with a distinct note of caution in her voice, "I don't know why some people do the bad things they do to other people, Johnisha."

I memorized the lyrics of "Missing You" and practiced with Diana on the radio.

Real Estate

Prior to third grade, I never thought too hard about what my father did for a living. I knew he left the house five days a week, and most nights we picked him up on the corner of 14th and T Streets NW, where he was a DC celebrity. Everybody knew Mr. Johnny, as he was called (by everyone except my mother, who called him John at home). There was always a regular buzz of people around him—men and occasionally women who seemed to be speaking a different language, unlike the precise diction my dad used at home. Watching him interact with these folks was like witnessing a different side of his personality, and it was one of my first lessons in code-switching. For the most part, I didn't understand their overly loud banter, but I picked up the emotion of it and whether it signified a good day or a bad one. Because I frequently listened to my parents' raised voices to predict whether violence would break out, I was good at discerning motives and moods, and I preferred quiet, gentle voices.

My dad's physicality was also different around these friends—his arms swung more liberally, his strut was more exaggerated, and he laughed with his mouth open. Some of my father's acquaintances would come up to the car to speak to my mother, lowering their decibels and addressing her deferentially as Ms. Lussia. She always greeted these men, including Mr. Reds, my dad's numbers writer, warmly.

Perhaps because of my dad's local celebrity, I started a running joke with my mother about him riding around in limousines with his girlfriend, a woman I named Francine Caloop. Francine had wavy auburn hair (likely because I was smitten with *Anne of Green Gables*) and was incredibly wealthy. Her wrists were draped in multiple jeweled bracelets, and she liked to wear sequined dresses to nighttime events. My mother played along with this fantasy, and any time we saw a limo in the city we would point to it and say, "There goes Francine Caloop. Maybe she's going to see the president or to the Four Seasons hotel!"

During these years, my mother was a homemaker and performed all the usual domestic duties, including shopping, cooking, cleaning, and bill paying (she even got my dad to sign up for an American Express card). She also kept the trains running when it came to shuttling Megan and me to our friends' houses, music lessons, orchestra practice, and other extracurricular activities.

By the time we moved away from Evarts Street, there were fewer of us, as my brothers had started to go their separate ways, including Adrin, who enlisted in the navy. At first I had to share a room with my sister, but this was an improvement over bunking with my parents. Eventually, when my last brother moved out, I was able to have a room of my own. My mother let me pick out new wallpaper—a print with bouquets of violets tied with purple ribbon—to replace the dull taupe design that looked like unblinking eyes in the middle of diamonds. The neighbors I met were still mostly Black and brown, and there were three other children around my age to play with. But there were also a lot more white people here than in our old neighborhood in Northeast DC.

My mother still entertained and cooked for my brothers whenever they showed up at the house solo or with their latest girlfriends. Over the years, I witnessed many of these girlfriends come and go, so I learned not to get too attached. My mother knew each brother's favorite dish—for instance, my brother Charles loved her lasagna. She would load them up with cake to take home or with their other favorite (and mine)—chocolate chip cookies. To protect our fair share from the boys, I often hid a few cookies away for Megan and myself whenever I heard the doorbell ring.

50   *The Graduate*

We were also visited by some of the people who inhabited my dad's U Street universe. My favorites were Mr. Al and Ms. Frances. Mr. Al had platinum hair, a more substantial mustache than my father's thin one, a portly frame, and a soft-spoken mien. He said little but smiled a lot. I recognized him as a man with a kind and gentle heart. His lady companion, Ms. Frances, had a similar body type, large tinted glasses, and a short S-curl. Her voice was like warm cinnamon tea on a chilly day, and she genuinely loved children—me in particular. She brought me all kinds of toys (even though my mother warned her not to spoil me) and then got down on the floor and played with me while the other adults did their own thing.

In addition, there were people like Mr. Jimmy C, who lived in a mansion (to my eyes) out in Potomac. Mr. Jimmy towered over me; his skin was as pale as my mother's, and his hair was just as straight. His wife was slightly darker (a light bronze); she clearly enjoyed makeup, and she had blonde streaks in her hair. Although they both looked white to nondiscerning eyes, as soon as Mr. Jimmy opened his mouth, you knew he was a soul brother. It turns out he was one of the best fences in the city and the source of some of my mother's finest attire. My father brought home his share of hot goods, including some elegant evening wear for my parents' date nights. In particular, there was one off-the-shoulder gown patterned in a mosaic of greens threaded with gold that I imagined myself growing into.

Like all my older siblings, I attended Catholic school, but my mother sent me to a different preschool: St. Ann's. According to Johnny, because of this choice and our move across town, some of the church folks at St. Augustine's thought the Matthews family might be getting a little uppity. Despite its location in the city's predominantly white Ward 3, my classmates at St. Ann's were mostly Black and brown. Many of the parents weren't American-born; they came from countries such as South Africa, Portugal, Kenya, and Guatemala, and some were in the diplomatic corps. One of the boys was biracial—like me, his father was Black and his mother was white.

After second grade, my mother pulled me and my sister out of Catholic school. She wanted us to be challenged academically. My mother had taught me my letters and rudimentary reading before I started at St. Ann's, and she was a volunteer reading tutor at the school. By first grade, I was the only one in my class allowed to browse and buy from the older kids' section at the school book fair. Both my sister and I were die-hard readers, but our personalities couldn't have been more different. Megan was always flapping off at the gums and making mischief just to get a little more attention, while I was happy to take my books or my sketchbooks and sit in the corner entertaining myself.

Sidwell Friends School was known for its excellent academic program and its liberal Quaker-based philosophy. It was a majority-white school with a cast of influential and powerful parents, including members of the president's cabinet and prominent lawyers, writers, scientists, journalists, and doctors. Many of the students lived in the moneyed and homogeneous neighborhoods of Georgetown, Cleveland Park, and Spring Valley in DC or Potomac and Bethesda in Maryland. Few came from a nontraditional blended family with interracial, interfaith parents.

At my new school, I had to contend with highly precocious children who asked what my father did for a living. No one at St. Ann's had ever asked me about my father's work, and besides, people from St. Ann's already knew our family. My grandmother was an extremely beloved churchgoer who participated in the social life of St. Augustine's, which was a stone's throw from her home. St. Augustine parishioners sent their kids to St. Ann's, and some of them taught there.

I was utterly unprepared for the prying at Sidwell, and I was troubled by my glaring ignorance. "Mom, what do I say when people ask me what Dad does?" I sheepishly asked, my arms crossed behind my back.

My mom was circumspect. "Well, you just tell them that your dad is in real estate."

I could tell her answer wasn't exactly what I wanted to know, but at least it was an answer. I did know that my dad owned

52   *The Graduate*

properties. After we moved, he kept the house on Evarts Street for a time. And he always seemed to be hanging around with a certain real estate agent, an old, light-skinned Black man who carried himself much more stiffly and formally than my father's other colleagues. What I failed to realize at the time but would appreciate as an adult was that working in the numbers game required you to navigate myriad spaces throughout the city—street corners, barbershops, convenience stores, and covert offices in apartment buildings. In this sense, Dad was very much involved in the real estate business.

Yet something didn't add up. And then one day I answered an unusual telephone call. The phone sat on a lacquered table under my favorite lamp—a porcelain woman with a green floral-print dress ballooning around her, her brunette hair styled in elegant finger waves. I picked up the phone, and a friendly but unfamiliar voice asked if my dad was available. He wasn't, and I told the caller so. The man responded by giving me a message: his name and the number he wanted my father to "play." An hour or so later, I scurried to give my dad the message as faithfully as I could.

The relaxed expression on my father's face instantly morphed. Although I had seen him angry countless times, this seemed more like anxiety combined with disbelief. "Don't ever, ever, ever take a call like that again. You hear me?" He didn't yell, but he overenunciated every word. I felt a frisson go through me. All those paper lottery slips, adding machines, decks of what my mother called "marked" cards, and the gleaming red and green dice (for craps games) stored beyond my reach on top of my parents' dresser I now recognized as part of my dad's work. This was what he was doing when we picked him up outside a small convenience store I was never allowed to enter. This was the work that tied him to Mr. Al and Ms. Frances and the grandfatherly men who visited our house in their perfectly maintained cars, brought us gifts, and deferred to my father's every word and whim. This was the work that made the money my dad kept tucked away in his mattress and other hiding spots around the house. And this was the source of the money his friends gave me as birthday presents, which I kept in a small black patent leather purse hidden in one of my doll boxes in the attic. My mother repeatedly told me that if you don't take care of your money, people will steal it from you.

Code-Switching

At Sidwell, I learned to both be and not be my authentic self. Once my mom clued me in to how my dad made a living, I erected a curtain around my family life, shielding as much of the backstage element as I could. In one sense, my parents had equipped me well for my new role as a member of the social elite. I had traveled to the Middle East as part of a youth orchestra, and I was used to attending theater productions and touring museum exhibits. My parents did not believe in leaving their children at home when they dined at upscale restaurants, so I could order confidently from a menu, navigate multiutensil place settings, and wait patiently to be served. When it came to arts and culture, nothing at Sidwell would faze me.

But when I was forced to negotiate questions about my dad's occupation, I realized that it would be unwise to share some information too widely. I knew intuitively that the consequences might be catastrophic if I didn't adhere to social norms and perform convincingly in my new role among the rich. My mother was careful about whose houses I could visit, and sleepovers were only an occasional occurrence. She didn't trust a lot of people with her only biological child. This was likely due to one disastrous experience with a babysitter when I was just a toddler. She left me with a woman who also performed some simple chores around the house, including ironing and laundry, but on this occasion, she had been instructed to do nothing but keep an eye on me.

"When I returned," Mom said, "you were sitting on the floor in a wet diaper trying to stick something into an electrical socket. And that was the end of that."

As selective as my mother was about my excursions to friends' houses, she was even choosier about who spent time at our house. I recall having exactly one sleepover that I hosted in sixth grade for two of my friends. I was so excited about this rare treat that I wanted everything to be perfect. My mother toted a fold-up cot from the basement and allowed us to sleep in the master bedroom. She let us go to Blockbuster and rent a horror flick, which we watched under the covers as we ate popcorn. I even asked whether there was any way to get closed-captioning for my friend who was deaf (there wasn't).

My best friend Karima was the youngest child of a large family who lived in the neighborhood. She too had transferred into Sidwell, and like me, she was a bit of a math geek and took accelerated classes. Throughout high school, we remained the only two Black girls in those classes. Unlike my parents, hers were white-collar professionals—an engineer and a pediatrician—but their divorce made her home life visibly imperfect, so I didn't feel like I had to impress her. Something about Karima had a calming effect on my dad too; he regularly greeted her with a corny singsong joke that she unfailingly laughed at: "Karima, have you seen her?"

Although I never told them about the violence that took place in my household, as we aged, my friends got smarter and more observant. A friend from middle school lived in a spacious, pristine home, and we mostly hung out at her house. On a few occasions, though, she visited me at my home. By this time, my parents were having financial difficulties, forcing them to neglect house repairs. All the bathrooms were in some state of disrepair—either the sinks or the toilets didn't work—and the kitchen tile was peeling back and showing its age. Most embarrassing was a long crack in the kitchen window resulting from one of my dad's outbursts. My friend and I were in the kitchen fixing a snack when she asked, "Hey, so what happened to the window over there?" I felt the color rise to my face and made up some inane excuse, like I had cracked the window by

56   *The Graduate*

throwing a softball. I certainly didn't admit that my dad had hit the window with his fist. When my friend came over again weeks or months later, the crack was still there, and she asked more out of curiosity than rudeness, "You still haven't gotten that fixed?" How do you explain to someone who lives in a beautiful home with a pool and a landscaped yard why you haven't fixed something as obvious as a broken window in your house?

While Sidwell created new complications for me, it also provided me with an essential outlet for my turmoil. I experienced the thrill and solace of writing creatively and cogently; I found a way to express myself when my voice had so often been stifled in daily life. My first creative writing experience came as a new third grader at Sidwell. I had written no more than a few sentences at a time for my Catholic school assignments, but suddenly my homework included recounting the legend of Gilgamesh and describing the advent of an agricultural society in Mesopotamia. Then one afternoon a solidly built, middle-aged brunette woman with a patient demeanor introduced herself as a creative writing instructor and asked us to produce poems that would be included in a student magazine.

The first assignment was to describe a family member as a statue. I chose my mother as the subject. My eraser burned through the paper as I attempted to come up with some suitably impressive words. I second-guessed myself not only about the words but also about where to put the line breaks. I had to feel my way through— kind of like sight-reading a violin piece for the first time. I thought of all the words I knew that conveyed richness and treasure and compared each part of my mom to those things:

> My mother would be a mother of pearl statue,
> Smooth and sparkling and shiny.
> Her hair would be strands of ebony silk
> With little bits of silver in it.
> Her eyes would be bright and shining emeralds
> Alert and having an aura as if they were smiling.

Gradually, the writing process became more natural and less painstaking, more pleasure than punishment. It also became a way to reincarnate my attic hideaway of long ago.

My eighth-grade English teacher probably had the most profound effect on my self-expression. Ms. Taylor (anyone who called her Mrs. or Miss would receive a piercing death glare) was a tall, brunette, deep-voiced Jewish woman (like my mother). She had a PhD in English, was a self-professed feminist, and was a divorcée with a teenage son. From the beginning of her classroom reign, it was clear she would not be blowing sunshine up the asses of any private-school parents. Accordingly, many of my classmates' parents appreciated neither Ms. Taylor nor her grading scale. Although her brusqueness was initially intimidating, there was something about her that I intuitively felt I could trust. Maybe it was because she wasn't afraid to cry in our presence out of anger or frustration when the boys in the class wouldn't behave. In contrast, I often cried out of fear and was terrified of what people would think of me.

My mother bought me a Smith Corona word processor that I kept on a roller shelf catty-corner from my four-poster bed. I was a proficient typist because Mom had signed me up for a summer typing class between sixth and seventh grades. The word processor was bulky, with a paperback-sized touch pad; the screen's lettering was as boxy as the machine itself. When I made a typo, I would have to manually apply white correction fluid, as the extremely noisy ink cartridge didn't always fully conceal the errors.

One fundamental piece of writing advice Ms. Taylor gave her students was to abandon the idea of achieving perfection the first time around. In doing so, she granted us license to be messy. She recommended turning off the word processor screen, or at least not looking at it, when typing the first iteration of our ideas: this allowed the ideas to take flight without being weighed down by the technicalities of punctuation, spelling, syntax, and structure. Those aspects of writing could be addressed later through editing and revision. For me, this was a revelation. I always tried to be a model student. Deep down, I thought that if I was smart enough and well-behaved enough, I could fend off the eruptions at home.

58   *The Graduate*

The fact that this strategy hadn't succeeded thus far didn't change my approach. I couldn't alter my family dynamics, but at least I could indulge myself in this one aspect of my existence. So I began to write with abandon, knowing no one but me would ever see the evidence of these wildly imperfect first drafts. I would turn off the screen, with its oversized green box of a cursor, and just follow my thoughts down every fanciful and improbable rabbit hole.

Beyond promoting this essential writing trick, Ms. Taylor was one of those people who viewed me differently from the way I saw myself. For one of my class assignments, I read and wrote about Cynthia Voight's young-adult novel *Dicey's Song*. In this sequel to *Homecoming*, the four Tillerman children are settling into the Eastern Shore home of their estranged grandmother, after being abandoned by their mother. The oldest, Dicey, who was my age, makes friends with Mina Smiths, a poised and self-possessed African American classmate and dancer. Mina manages to break through Dicey's hard shell with her charm and unwavering loyalty. When Ms. Taylor returned my paper on *Dicey's Song*, she said offhandedly, "You know, when I picture Mina in my head, I see you, Johnisha." I mumbled my thanks and most assuredly blushed.

In my free time, I regularly read books—both fiction and nonfiction—written by Black authors and with Black characters, but it was uncommon for me to share a racial identity with any of the characters I encountered in the books I read for English class. Mina was a standout for this reason, and she was someone I aspired to be. She wasn't afraid to deviate from what people expected of a Black girl, dismissing the criticism of her Black friends for befriending a "honky." She was also uncowed by bullies of the adolescent or adult variety. Meanwhile, I lived with my biggest tormentor: my father. I had not yet found the voice or the means to stand up to his verbal and physical abuse of my mother. At the same time, I was being harassed by my Black male classmates for not fitting their specific mold of Blackness. (In contrast, I was friends with most of the Black girls, who didn't seem to take issue with my differences. This sisterhood would persist throughout the decades.) One of the boys in my art class repeatedly called me Oreo (black on the outside, white on the inside) and mocked my speech because it sounded "too white" to his ears. Two other Black boys in my French class made conspicuous quacking sounds because my feet turned out at forty-five-degree angles, a minor but sometimes painful birth defect that an orthopedic surgeon told me should have been corrected in infancy. This harassment by my racial peers bruised my heart in ways that the microaggressions of white students and their families could not. In my mind, we "belonged" to each other, as people of color always do when they find themselves marooned in an almost exclusively white environment. Therefore, when Ms. Taylor said she saw me as Mina or Mina as me, I was more than a little surprised. It made me feel beautiful, hopeful, and resilient. It made me feel all the things I didn't feel most days of my preteen life.

Ironically, the biggest bully in my life ended the cycle of intimidation at school. I had finally reached the breaking point and pleaded hysterically with my parents to let me stay home from school the next day. I told my mother I had violent thoughts and feared what might happen if the situation continued. I had rejected my parents' initial offer to call the ringleader's parents, which I thought would lead to reprisal and make my life even more intolerable. The solution we came up with was to have my dad monitor the situation on the ground, so he posted himself outside my art classroom.

When it came to Sidwell, my dad was generally hands off. As a previously single father, he had already served his time participating in PTA activities. And he found some of the other parents off-putting—both white and Black. The white parents seemed too self-important, and about the Black parents he sneered, "I don't need to spend time with those Jack and Jill motherfuckers," referring to a Black social and civic organization whose members were "professionals," unlike my parents.[1] The Black parents likely hit a nerve from his La Plata days with the we-sorts, and he felt the disdain the Black DC establishment had for those who operated in the informal economy.

However, when someone or something (other than himself) threatened the well-being of his children, my father was a bulwark.

60   *The Graduate*

He stepped up no matter the cost or the inconvenience. It was an admirable trait, but at times, he went too far. "When Dad was younger, he was a lot meaner," my brother Michael told me after our father's memorial service. In temperament, Michael was probably the sibling most like me. He was sensitive, quiet, and cautious, but also a bit mischievous. He was the Matthews golden boy; he excelled academically, was the first Black president of his high school class, and got a job as an engineer at IBM out of college in the 1980s. "I'll never forget," he said. "I was very little, and I had been out playing ball in the street, and one of the neighborhood teenagers took the ball away from me. I went in the house to tell Dad, and he ran out there and hit the boy so hard, he gushed blood out of his nose. I was stunned." Clearly, the episode still haunted Michael all these years later.

If I had heard Michael's story earlier, I might not have agreed to my dad's offer to stand guard outside my classroom. But at the time, I trusted him. I had to. (I also knew from experience that my father's death glare was enough to scare someone straight.) However, my dad was not noisy or disruptive. The surprisingly stoic manner in which he watched over me was powerful evidence of his love—a love I didn't feel on a day-to-day basis, though I desperately craved it. And because of that day, I finally summoned the courage to report the students to the school counselor. She and the principal intervened, sending my tormentors a strong message to stop or face suspension. It seemed that my father had saved the day.

South Pacific

At thirteen years old, I had never been kissed by a boy, except on-stage as part of the cast of the Rodgers and Hammerstein musical *South Pacific*. I loved musical theater, and my soprano voice was well suited for these roles. But when I was selected to play Liat, the exotic island girl, I was appalled at the idea of standing before an entire audience with a boy from my math class playing a bare-chested Lieutenant Cable. What would my father think of me?

During early rehearsals, our dynamic drama teacher was focused on us learning our songs and memorizing our dialogue. Because my character didn't speak English (other than when she sang—an adaptation made for our particular production), I had few words to memorize. For the most part, I was supposed to stand there and look appealing. By dress rehearsals, it was time to practice the kiss, and I panicked. "You can't put it off any longer, Johnisha," my teacher admonished as her patience began to wear thin. The night before the first rehearsal of the kiss, I briefly contemplated dropping out of the production, but I knew that would create undue hardship for the teacher and the rest of the cast. On the day of rehearsal, I gulped back huge sobs; my throat was tight, and hot salty tears cut rivulets in my cheeks. The boy playing Cable was crestfallen. I overheard him whisper, "She must really hate me." But it wasn't that.

I was thinking of my father and his sense of Catholic uprightness, at least when it came to the young women in our family. My father admired the intelligence of his daughters. He supported all

62 *The Graduate*

our ambitions, including my aspiration to become a pediatrician. One day, he brought home a mysterious object in a scuffed black case. I watched with curiosity as he unlatched the clasp to reveal a red velvet interior cradling an ancient microscope, complete with slides. He had discovered it at one of his friend's pawnshops. I thought it was better than any of the brand-new presents I had received. A huge grin spread across my face. "Wow, Dad, I love it!" I exclaimed.

However, matters of the body were very different from matters of the brain. With the exception of Michael, my brothers were not academically inclined, and when it came to the opposite sex, they were allowed to weave tangled webs of infidelities. Not so my father's daughters. Boys who came to see us were either driven away or forced to remain downstairs where they could be supervised. My father even restricted my TV viewing to prohibit anything even remotely sexual. "What is that smut you're watching?" he'd complain when movie characters got passionate or Bobby Brown fondled his crotch while dancing to "My Prerogative" on MTV. The moment I heard the slightest creak of his foot on the basement stairs, I'd switch the channel to something tame such as the local news.

As I grew, so did my dad's suspicion of me. Maybe this was a projection of his own sordid relationship history, although I was not aware of him cheating on my mother. Every time I wore a skirt or a dress, he asked me whether I had a slip on underneath. Although I was now about five foot two, with the beginnings of curves, I was still slender and flat-chested enough to wear Carter's camisoles, which I called undershirts. I could see that no one else in the school locker room wore undershirts. If they didn't wear bras, they scoffed at tradition and went braless, their burgeoning chests either pinned down or flying free. I never used the showers in the gym locker room or paraded my wet naked buttocks up and down the rows of lockers, like many of my classmates did. Whenever I changed, I found ways to obscure my body.

My friend Karima and I fantasized about various movie stars—mostly biracial or racially ambiguous people (like me) such as Keanu Reeves, Russell Wong, Mario Van Peebles, and Shemar Moore. I was not considered attractive in my school, which was filled with predominantly white girls with long, straight hair and light-colored eyes. No boys ever liked me the way I liked them, but my dad didn't know he had no need to worry. And even if a boy did like me, I would have been way too scared to bring him home.

The weekend of the performance of *South Pacific*, my dad brought me a bouquet of long-stemmed red roses. He never mentioned the moment I had obsessed over for weeks. I wondered if perhaps my mom had prepared him for the kissing scene. I was relieved but also perplexed.

A week or two later at school, Lieutenant Cable's mother handed me an envelope with my name scrawled on the front. When I got home, I removed the envelope full of photos from my backpack. My face grew warm as I flipped through my scenes from the play and photos of the whole cast. The latter I kept; the former I ripped up.

"Father, Father, We Don't Need to Escalate"

"I will call the police if you don't fucking stop it!" My parents and I were in the kitchen. My father had his hands curled around my mother's throat as he pinned her in the corner closest to the back door. He had used this maneuver innumerable times to put her in her place and stifle her. But he was nearly seventy years old now and lacked the stamina of a younger man. Still, he could be dangerous.

In some far corner of my brain, I knew my outburst might make things worse. I had no one to back me up. I was only fourteen years old, closing in on the same height as my mother but slighter, at around 110 pounds. My voice was so shrill and fearless it felt disconnected from my body. But who else could it have been?

Miraculously, my verbal threat was effective. My heart was thrumming in my ears as my father paused and seemed to look through me, his eyes glazed as if he were in a trance. Perhaps he was having some sort of out-of-body experience himself during this fit of violence; or maybe he was astounded that I would actually summon the Metropolitan Police Department to the scene. I was unaware of his history with the police at the time, and I lacked the perspective and knowledge to consider the different type of danger posed when the police intervened in Black families. I was, quite simply, desperate for the violence against my mother to stop—immediately. Regardless of the precise reason why, my father relinquished his

"Father, Father, We Don't Need to Escalate"   65

grip and quietly stepped away, without an apology or any other utterance. It would not be the last time he assaulted my mother, but it was the first time I knew I could defend her if I had to.

My appreciation for Marvin Gaye's music had started years ago, listening to oldies radio stations in the car with my mom. Each year, Howard University's radio station, WHUR, produced a tribute to Gaye in honor of his birthday. He had been born in DC and was only a year younger than my mother. The tribute program covered Marvin's transformation from an aspirational crooner to the Prince of Soul. It discussed his bitter divorce and how he took revenge in the form of the alimony album *Here, My Dear*, which was critically acclaimed in spite of his attempt to tank it. And it celebrated him as the conscience and griot of a generation when it came to his most enduring contribution to popular music, the 1971 album *What's Going On?* But for me, it was Marvin's relationship with his father and how his life ended that I connected to. Marvin died because he jumped into a fight between his father, Marvin Sr., and his mother, Alberta. Marvin Sr. shot his famous offspring three times with a gun his son had given him.

Marvin's most famous composition, "What's Going On?" was the antiwar anthem the country needed during Vietnam. But was there a subtext? Were those lines about a mother crying and his plea "Father, Father, we don't need to escalate" Marvin's way of speaking to his parents? Marvin allegedly told a friend during the last month of his life, "I have just one father. I want to make peace with him." It was rumored that the closest thing to "I love you" Marvin Sr. had ever said to his son was that he "didn't dislike him." Marvin Jr. suffered from severe depression as an adult, and his cocaine addiction likely sprang from an effort to self-medicate. He died on the day before his forty-fifth birthday, when his luck ran out and his fame could not shield him from his father's anger. Beautiful Marvin, with his sweet tenor voice that sounded like a prayer. Beautiful Marvin, who was tired of abuse. Beautiful Marvin, who tried to be a hero. Beautiful Marvin, who was gone. How could his fate not haunt me? It was like a Shakespearean tragedy.

Kingdom Come

It is a summer night before my fifteenth birthday, and I am wedged between my parents in the carmine belly of the Kennedy Center for Performing Arts watching Richard Eyre's production of Shakespeare's *Richard III*. My father is rapt, his eyes glued to the stage, following every tiny movement of the eponymous character and the rest of the acting company. For him, my mother and I have faded away, at least until intermission snaps him back to the present and he can't wait to discuss Richard's machinations with us. Richard is more like a viper than the boar (which is his emblem), at least the way British thespian Sir Ian McKellen plays him. The character speaks from both sides of his mouth—one side puffed up with flattery and praise for his kin, his words conveying duty and honor on the surface, while the other side drips with vile dishonor and dissemblance for the benefit of his fellow plotters and for us, the captive audience.

For almost as long as I can remember, my father kept the slim black and red New Temple volumes of Shakespeare's *Richard III*, *King Lear*, *Othello*, and *Julius Caesar* in a magazine rack by his bed, along with miscellaneous copies of *Time* and my mother's old *National Geographic* issues (she collected the maps). He reread the plays often, as evidenced by the dog-eared pages. He was especially fond of *Othello*, a vastly conflicting tragedy featuring the consummate (and Black) outsider. Othello is a man both "dignified" and "self-possessed," of obvious use to the Venetians for his military prowess as they simultaneously scorn his undesirable Black visage and his "lusty" desire for the white Desdemona. During Shakespeare's time, Jacobean audiences were already well acquainted with writings such as Leo Africanus's, which equated Blackness with extreme jealousy.[1]

Despite the play's troubling racial tropes[2]—which likely buttressed the myth of the sexual Black predator used to justify lynching—my father found something deeply worthy and relatable in this maligned and misunderstood character. In some ways, he saw himself in Othello. Like my father, the Moor is a man who has "done the state some service" and, at least until his enemies begin to plot against him and he gradually loses his rationality, his supreme eloquence is a defining and admirable characteristic.[3]

To my great irritation, my father equated the serious study of literature with Shakespeare, to the exclusion of many other worthy writers who resembled us physically and shared our experiences as Black Americans. I was more interested in celebrating the rich canon of brilliant Black writers, especially women writers such as Zora Neale Hurston, Toni Morrison, Gloria Naylor, Maya Angelou, and Alice Walker. Given this difference in generational perspective, I was initially skeptical of Shakespeare. Would I find the language incomprehensible? Would I need a dictionary to decipher it? And what did my father find so compelling about the plays that made him read them again and again? But on that night at the Kennedy Center, I began to understand my dad's love affair with Shakespeare.

For that production of *Richard III*, the audience was transported to 1930s Europe: the scheming Richard, Duke of Gloucester, is a hardened and crippled military strategist and spiritual kinsman to Adolf Hitler, willing to dispose of any and all foes to achieve his ultimate ambition—the British throne. The production's staging was a spectacle of smoke and shadow, accented by the red of Reich-style pageantry and banners carrying Richard's emblem (the boar). Eyre wanted the audience to anticipate Hitler's rise, so his staging reflected the frightful Nuremberg rallies. It all seemed a bit eerie to me and vastly affecting, especially as a Jewish child who had read

68 *The Graduate*

pretty widely about the horrors of the Holocaust. What I didn't think about at the time was how this production echoed my father's own experience as a World War II veteran fighting the very fascism the play addressed head-on.

At the pivotal moment in the fifth and final act, Richard, the usurper, has run out of yes-men to do his bidding. Cornered by the Duke of Richmond's forces, he has nowhere to turn. He is moments from death as he utters the most famous lines in the play, a desperate prayer for an equine savior:

> I have set my life upon a cast
> And I will stand the hazard of the die. . . .
> A horse, a horse, my kingdom for a horse!

His voice cracks with the desperation of imminent and fatal defeat.

Richard's dreams are blasted. All the curses heaped upon him have come true; all his schemes have gone awry with the toss of a die. It is a sixteenth-century play adapted to twentieth-century issues with a villain so clever that at times you must chuckle along with him.

After this immersion, I became better acquainted with Shakespeare's work through my high school English classes. I depended heavily on annotations to appreciate the allusions, syntax, double entendres, and stage directions. When I admitted to my father that I enjoyed the challenge of the language, he called me "a chip off the old block."

As an English literature major in college, I encountered more Shakespeare and eventually became more comfortable with the language, using the context to inform my understanding. I gradually allowed the characters and the words to speak to me directly and didn't rely so heavily on the notes and commentary in my Norton anthology or the *Oxford English Dictionary*. Shakespeare, after all, wrote for ordinary people and the popular theater. His work is bawdy and irreverent and sometimes downright silly, even the tragedies. I have also found myself pondering more and more how a character's actions and words are often mismatched, from Othello's standard-bearer Iago to the bastard Edmund in *King Lear*. But what I have retained from my reading is something more essential—that Shakespeare isn't so figuratively distant from the world I inhabit. I recognize characters with the same twisted motives and hubris, manifesting the same rapid reversals and regrets, as my father. And when I look back on the night of that Kennedy Center performance, I wonder: Could he see the writing on the wall? Was he aware that the crumbling of Richard's kingdom was in some ways analogous to the decline of his street numbers business?

My father kept his numbers business afloat until the mid-1990s, when I was finishing high school. Although he was indefatigable, tough, and even relentlessly cruel whether he needed to be or not, he was not a cold-blooded mercenary, a cheater, or a purveyor of death like the Duke of Gloucester. Perhaps if he had been, he could have hung on longer. Instead, he ended up broke, on the brink of losing both his house and his sanity.

By the time he was released from the Lorton in 1977, the numbers game was already evolving. States were looking for new revenue streams amidst the economic hardship and antitax sentiment of the 1970s. One proposed solution was to legalize a form of gambling that many considered relatively harmless in comparison to other so-called vice crimes—one that Black people played a substantial role in perfecting. It came as no surprise to many numbers operators that the government cast a covetous eye on their lucrative venture. As early as the 1950s, successful Nashville club owner and numbers banker William "Sou" Bridgeforth "wondered how long before the government . . . could profit from the lottery racket."[4]

Segments of the public supported the legalization of gambling for various reasons. "Many white voters . . . supported legalization because they thought state-run gambling would primarily attract Black numbers players, who would then foot the bill for services that those white voters didn't want to pay for anyway, such as better schools in urban areas they had lately fled. . . . Meanwhile, many [Black] voters supported legalization because they believed that it would ease their friction with the police, for whom numbers games had long served as a reason . . . to interrogate and imprison people of color."[5]

Maryland launched a state lottery in 1973; by 1980, DC residents were spending more than $30 million a year buying lottery tickets in that neighboring state. Consequently, DC officials decided it would be wise to secure some of those funds for their own needs, including education, recreation and parks, public safety, housing, and senior and child services. By 1983, seventeen states and the District of Columbia were operating legal lotteries.

Initially, the DC Lottery was slow to catch on with bettors, and street numbers remained vastly more popular and profitable. "DC police officials estimate[d] that the city's illegal numbers industry [was] enjoying gross revenues of up to $250 million a year. . . . By comparison, the D.C. Lottery Board [had] grossed about $54 million since it started operating [in August 1982]. D.C. lottery officials [said] they expect[ed] the city to gross $100 million from the planned legal numbers game in its first year of operation."[6]

I was surprised to discover from newspaper accounts that my father was arrested again in 1983, along with his running partner. The search for more details about this arrest resulted in a factual dead end (none of the legal files I received were connected to this arrest), but coverage in the *Washington Post* revealed how successful my dad's numbers outfit remained: "D.C. Police announced yesterday that a five-month investigation has resulted in the arrest on lottery charges of three people alleged to head one of the city's biggest illegal numbers operations, thought to take in about $30,000 a day. . . . 'We believe this is one of the top five illegal lottery organizations in the city,' said Sgt. Carnwell Dean, of the department's gambling squad. 'It's a multimillion-dollar-a-year operation.'"[7]

Street numbers still offered significant advantages that loyal, old-time bettors were loath to forfeit. For instance, if a bettor had a good reputation with his or her banker, the bettor could keep a number in play without having to pay up—a "customer service" the DC Lottery didn't offer. Although it was customary to give the banker a "tip" or commission, the banker would hand-deliver the money, whereas legal bettors had to go to DC Lottery headquarters to collect their winnings. Plus, street bettors didn't have to worry about paying taxes on their winnings.

However, the legal lotteries in DC, Maryland, and Virginia soon began to offer enticements that couldn't be matched by the humble street lottery. Some bettors preferred not having to wait for the results of the various horse races to come in—they could find out the winning number instantaneously. State lotteries also employed clever and aggressive Madison Avenue marketing strategies to attract customers.[8] Because of competition from neighboring jurisdictions, lottery officials recognized that they needed to constantly promote and change their products to at least maintain if not grow sales. Lotteries experience "a series of starts, stops, and regressions" due to "'jackpot fatigue'—the fate of games that attract less and less attention." To counter this betting fatigue, the state lotteries invested huge sums in advertising campaigns, focus groups, polls, and psychographic studies.[9] Jackpots grew bigger, especially with the advent of rollover jackpot games like Lotto. State lotteries also created a menu of betting options tailored to appeal to stereotypes about different groups. Because it was believed that women lost interest more quickly than men, officials enticed them with colorful scratch-off tickets. Players with "fragile egos" allegedly needed faster games with more prizes. Studies characterized Pick 3 players as "superstitious" individuals who played the same numbers religiously and were "less educated, lower income and more black than players overall."[10] The DC Lottery offerings include two-, three-, four-, and five-digit games, as well as Powerball, Mega Millions, Lucky for Life, and DC Scratchers.

The street numbers adapted its elegantly choreographed betting scheme to accommodate the new reality of the legal lottery. These modifications included switching the source of its winning numbers from horse races to the legal lottery. My father and his colleagues were forced to play the DC Lottery themselves to backstop any large bets in their own lottery. For example, if one of his customers placed a large bet on a certain combination, my father played that same combination through the DC Lottery so that he could use his winnings to pay off his street bettor. Increasingly, he brought home piles of those white paper squares with the pinkish-red stripe issued by the DC Lottery and slapped them down on his bedroom desk at the end of the workday.

Ironically, it was the DC Lottery that rendered betting visible in our home. In addition to backstopping street bets, my father played his sentimental favorites with the DC Lottery—209, which was the apartment building where he had lived with Judy, and 1439, our house number. My mother, in contrast, was more enamored with the instant gratification of cheap scratch-offs, as well as the enormous jackpots of Lotto and Powerball. She'd buy scratch tickets at the Silver Spring 7-Eleven and toss them to me as I sat next to her in the front seat of the car. I'd pick up a quarter and go to town, scratching off the silver coating to reveal our potential prizes. "Nothing this time," I announced glumly on the innumerable occasions when our luck brought us nothing but the silver shavings I carefully trailed out the open car window.

With their debts piling up, it was no wonder that my parents were lured by the unfathomably large jackpots, despite the impossible odds. My mother stood in line to purchase a combination of preselected and computer-generated numbers for Powerball. To make her selections, she would fill out a card, choosing five numbers between 1 and 59 and a single Powerball number between 1 and 26. I often kept her company, and we would daydream about what we would do if we won. We were never too greedy or extravagant. "I'd just like to be able to get out of debt, send you to college, and maybe have a nice vacation house," my mother mused, a faraway look in her eyes. The letdown of losing was always hard when the numbers were released and our dreams evaporated.

The DC Lottery also entered our home through the televised drawings. My parents and I would tune in right before my favorite primetime shows to see a host announce the night's winning numbers. The numbers were selected from among several ping-pong-sized balls that rapidly rotated and bounced around in their plexiglass enclosure.

Kingdom Come 73

My parents weren't the only ones who became increasingly entwined with the DC Lottery. The numbers operators who were best able to insulate themselves from the lottery's financial impact did so by diversifying their business interests and actually becoming licensed DC Lottery agents. Some of my dad's peers owned and operated legal businesses such as liquor stores and convenience stores, while others were involved in the trafficking of drugs or guns. Liquor stores and convenience stores served as the backbone for lottery sales, especially in Black and brown neighborhoods; their owners earned approximately 5 percent on each lottery ticket sold.[11]

My dad didn't own any stores, and although his relationship with alcohol was unhealthy, he would never sell drugs to his community—not even to support his family. In his book, just about the worst thing you could do was take or sell drugs.

But crack cocaine would soon dominate the underground economy. DC had a robust heroin trade in the 1960s and 1970s, but cocaine and its cheaper derivative, crack, would devastate and decimate the city. Incarceration of Black and brown men skyrocketed due to a 100-to-1 sentencing disparity between crimes related to crack (associated with Black and brown communities and falsely assumed to be more addictive) and those involving cocaine (associated with rich white communities). In practical terms, a person possessing just 5 grams of crack was sentenced to the same term as someone possessing 500 grams of cocaine. The new kingpins of this sector were younger, richer, and more ruthless, and they lacked the honor code of my father's generation of hustlers. The old hustlers used violence as a last resort to enforce order, but the new ones were cold-blooded and employed it as a first response. As a result, by 1985, DC surpassed all US cities in per capita drug arrests. In 1991 the murder rate in DC peaked at 482, earning the city the unenviable nickname of murder capital of the nation. Open-air drug markets proliferated, and the resulting violence found its way into most neighborhoods.

The most legendary figure in DC's drug trade got his start in the numbers business. Rayful Edmond III had a direct connection to Colombia's Cali cartel and was DC's version of *The Wire*'s drug kingpin Avon Barksdale. Edmond's father, "Big Ray" Edmond Jr., was originally a numbers runner who "dabbled" in the drug trade. After the lottery significantly cut into Big Ray's income stream, he turned to importing cocaine and then taught his son the trade.[12] Rayful eventually surpassed his father and built a sophisticated drug smuggling, production, and retail operation. He became the poster boy for the city's war on drugs. Thus, the drug-running progeny of one aggrieved numbers runner terrorized DC. The transition between these two generations of a family is apt, considering that "prior to the war on drugs . . . gambling was the principal site of racially targeted policing in urban America."[13]

The decline of the street numbers business also corresponded with dramatic changes in the U Street–Shaw neighborhood—changes that originated in the tumultuous events of 1968. When my dad first arrived in DC in the 1940s, the area was described as the place "where you put your finery on." It was "the locus of D.C.'s middle- and upper-class black culture," with more than "three hundred black-owned businesses and organizations."[14] But when Martin Luther King Jr. was assassinated, Black people in DC (and elsewhere across the nation) expressed their outrage over the country's false promises and its unending violence against its Black citizenry. During four days of civil unrest, 1,352 private businesses were damaged and destroyed, about 5,000 jobs were lost, and more than 2,000 people were left newly homeless in DC.[15] This once segregated yet prideful and self-sufficient community suffered mightily in the aftermath of the 1968 riot, and the neighborhood received no help to aid its recovery. "Left behind were hundreds of burned-out buildings, whole blocks that looked as though they had been bombed into oblivion, vital centers of commerce for black Washington that had been reduced to rubble, [and] small business[es] and lifetimes of investment by their owners that had been obliterated."[16] Black residents who owned houses in or near the riot corridors experienced a marked decline in the median value of their properties, which severely impacted the intergenerational transfer of wealth. The riots increased insurance premiums and contributed to unemployment, crime, and poverty.

The neighborhood remained in this condition throughout most of my childhood. To those who had never experienced its glory firsthand or who lived outside its perimeters, it acquired a reputation for "prostitution, open-air drug markets, X-rated bookstores, and peep shows."[17] But for my family, it was still home. My grandmother lived in the neighborhood for decades, and after she died, my older sister Marilyn continued to reside in the house my dad had originally purchased for his mother on 15th Street.

My mother and I regularly traversed 14th Street on our way to pick up my father each night. I would stare out the windows and try to imagine what had once been. I didn't understand why the city was content to let the buildings remain as they stood—husks allowed to fester, boarded up, graffitied, and abandoned. My mother didn't have an answer for me, but she would regale me with stories of a bygone era, including how the old Tivoli Theater—located in the adjacent neighborhood of Columbia Heights—used to look in its heyday. It opened in 1924 (the same year my father was born), and for the next four decades the picture house was a crown jewel of the city. An advertisement in the *Washington Post* boasted that the Tivoli was "unsurpassed in beauty by any similar enterprise in the country," with a "foyer, lounging and smoking rooms notable for their richness of furnishings and exquisite décor," and a $35,000 pipe organ.[18] Black people weren't allowed to patronize the Tivoli until the 1950s, and even then the NAACP and other advocates had to pressure the theater to integrate its orchestra seats so that Black people weren't relegated to the balcony. No doubt this injustice was part of the long-simmering anger that resulted in the Tivoli and surrounding businesses becoming targets of the 1968 riots that followed King's assassination. The neighborhood's decline eventually forced the theater to close its doors the year before I was born. Although I was too young to recognize that this pattern was replicated across the nation, I did notice that these conditions affected only

76   *The Graduate*

the Black neighborhoods in DC. I didn't see any derelict properties in the neighborhoods where my wealthy friends lived.

Old-timers like my dad were faithful to the U Street neighborhood and did not abandon the businesses, the community, their clientele, or their cultural home, but developers had plans for U Street that would exclude many of its original inhabitants. This scenario has played out time and time again as urban centers with significant Black populations become targets of gentrification (a term that implies better days, but for whom?) and the Black residents are displaced by more affluent and usually white faces.

It is hard to pinpoint the exact moment things began to change for the old inhabitants of U Street, but 1986 was a pivotal year. That was when our infamous and wildly popular mayor Marion Barry attempted to revitalize the corridor using the Frank Reeves Center for Municipal Affairs on 14th and U Streets as a launch site. Ironically, the Reeves Center, which is one of the only buildings on lower U Street that I still recognize today, would house the DC Lottery headquarters, along with other government functions.

Throughout the remainder of the decade and into the 1990s, the neighborhood's demographics also shifted, facilitated by the opening of a new subway stop in the neighborhood. U Street–Shaw was newly invaded by middle- and upper-class home buyers, while losing many of its low- and moderate-income Black households. By the 2000s, as more white people moved into the neighborhood, home values rose, and luxury condominiums and apartments increased their rents. Upscale furniture stores and food markets, including Whole Foods and Trader Joe's, opened their doors. During my high school and college years, I observed the complexion and wealth of the neighborhood gradually change.

Along with this redevelopment, the small businesses owned by my dad's peers, such as blues bars and convenience stores, began to disappear. The proprietors could no longer pay the skyrocketing rents, their new neighbors had no desire to patronize their businesses, and landlords had other plans for the spaces. Thus, many of the original carriers and transmitters of the neighborhood's history were no longer visible or present to tell their stories. As they aged and died, their families could no longer afford the property taxes, and some were forced to sell their family homes. Marilyn eventually lost my grandmother's house. It is now occupied by a queer white couple who paid homage to the neighborhood's history with their own research and restoration efforts. It sits next to the Milk Bar, a franchise of a New York bakery, which replaced a used car lot.

Given these catastrophic changes to the Black world of U Street, I ask myself: Was the loss of my dad's livelihood ultimately the city's gain? After all, the purpose of the DC Lottery was ostensibly to provide money for additional services. The reality is far from clear-cut. With the displacement of the street lotteries and Black-owned businesses, many of the Black dollars that once circulated within Black communities no longer do. In other cities with street lotteries, activists advocated for a lottery model based on community control, allowing the affected communities to allocate the money to address their most pressing problems through local boards. However, these efforts were defeated.[19] As a result, even when lottery money is allocated to meet constituents' needs, the influx of funds is offset by legislators cutting the program's budget. This means that the greater the lottery windfall for public education, for instance, the deeper the cuts to the education budget.[20]

Within the District of Columbia, the lottery credits itself with paying a total of $2.3 billion over its lifetime to the DC general fund for constituent services. However, it regularly pays out more than 50 percent of its annual sales in prize money, and less than a quarter goes to the general fund. The remainder is used to pay for contractors' fees, advertising, agents' commissions, and sports wagering.[21] What's more, the big business of state lotteries functions as a regressive funding scheme by putting a disproportionate revenue-generating burden on the communities and people that can least afford it: "those making less than thirty thousand dollars spend thirteen percent" of their annual income on the lottery, as opposed to the 1 percent spent by individuals making more than $50,000 a year.[22] Everything about the lottery—the ad campaigns, the look of the tickets, and the math behind it—is designed to keep people playing. It is no wonder that the lottery is now a $91 billion business in America, with the most frequent bettors seeing little material gain.

Despite my dad's wit and grit, he couldn't compete with a behemoth. Like the culture of the neighborhood where he hustled, he was supplanted. The environment where he had once thrived was now inhabited by strangers who looked past him, without a thought or a greeting. At the end of each day, he placed his hands in emptier and emptier suit pockets.

Insufficient Funds

By my first year of high school in 1991–92, my father was experiencing a full-out financial crisis. He owed money to usurious lenders, and our house was in danger of being seized. On top of that, he paid off a $20,000 debt to a drug dealer who had threatened my brother's life. When the drug dealer heard that my dad was going to assume the debt but needed some time to come up with the funds, he said, "Mr. Johnny can have the time because I know he's good to his word."

But Mr. Johnny was now nearly seventy years old and without savings, a retirement fund, or a pension. He no longer had stashes of cash hidden under his mattress or in the closet. My mother took on two jobs to help pay down the spiraling debt—working days at her brother's deli and nights and weekends at a department store. I would see her for only an hour or two between jobs or if I took a bus to meet her during her lunch or dinner breaks.

My father took these events as a sign of catastrophic failure: his concept of fatherhood was defined primarily by the ability to support his family financially. He began to spend more time in bed, and he stopped eating regularly. He was frail and exhausted, wandering around the house in his black and white striped bathrobe—utterly unlike the indomitable man I'd grown up with. He stayed in his bedroom during the early evening, but at night his unrelenting insomnia led him to descend the stairs and sit at the

80   *The Graduate*

glass dining room table, reading and pondering. I found my fear of him metamorphosing into pity.

Something unexpected happened during this time: he had longer moments of approachability and lovability. I could talk to him more easily about the contours of his life, especially about his boyhood in La Plata. Like Shakespeare's King Lear, he became "less a figurehead and locked into authority, and more a person with a growing awareness of himself as a subject. . . . [It became easier] to appreciate him as a uniquely valuable 'person,' even as politically he is reduced to nothing."[1]

Prior to high school, we had enjoyed fleeting moments of connection. On Sundays, I liked to walk with him on the track at the nearby Carter Barron complex on the fringe of Rock Creek Park, and when I was learning to play tennis, he would hit balls with me on the courts there. When I was in middle school, he and I watched NBA games together, and he patiently answered all my questions about both our favorite and our loathed Lakers, Celtics, and Bulls players. We rooted for James Worthy, a serious brother who lived up to his reputation as a seven-time NBA all-star and three-time champion. His oversized goggles made Worthy easily identifiable running, jumping, and skirmishing on the court. We mutually ridiculed the bumbling Kurt Rambis, who resembled a big shaggy sheepdog and was just about as aerodynamic and graceful as one. During the games, especially when our teams were winning, my father allowed me a few celebratory sips of his cold, bitter Heineken. We'd usually be doing something else while watching TV to keep our hands busy, like snapping string beans for Sunday dinner or cracking pecans and walnuts to snack on. The taste of those nuts still brings to mind spending time with my father—me using the two-pronged nutcracker, and him using his teeth to break the nuts open, despite my mom's admonishments.

My dad and I were also united in our enthusiasm for the card game Tonk, which I don't think any of my rummy- or spades-playing classmates at Sidwell had ever heard of. It represented my father's past, for it was played both in military barracks and among the great Black blues and jazz musicians, including DC native Duke

Ellington and his orchestra. Occasionally, I covertly examined the "marked" poker decks on Dad's bureau, but poker represented the exclusive world of high-stakes gambling. Tonk was more my speed.

Tonk was easily played with two people and a standard deck of cards. The goal was to be the first to discard your cards (always dealt in odd numbers) by forming them into spreads—either three or four same-numbered cards or three or more consecutively numbered cards of the same suit. As we played more and more often, usually at night, I became familiar with the complexities of the game and the vocabulary of "hits" and "tonking out." If I lost a game, my dad would look at my cards and gently offer some advice: "Here, you could have made this move instead. See how you could have gotten a spread here if you used your jack instead of going for the identical cards of different suits?" Eventually, I improved and won about half the time. Almost every time that happened I would ask, "Dad, did you let me win?" With an earnest look on his face he would respond, "No, ma'am." I didn't always believe him because I knew my dad was as much of a card shark as he was a numbers man.

But my father was no longer the sharp and confident betting man I had always known. I had never seen him so defeated, so fragile. I could tell he needed some special attention, and I didn't mind giving it. I often bounced on the rickety frame of my parents' antique bed, acting like a much younger child, and begged my dad to tell me stories from his childhood. "Okay," he'd say in his rich baritone. He wore V-neck undershirts to sleep, and I could smell the baby oil he rubbed into his skin after he showered. I could tell he liked having someone listen to him because his jaw would unclench and his eyes would spark. Sometimes he started with the tale of Teekittyko,[2] a story passed down from my great-grandmother Lizzie. Teekittyko was a creature so big and ugly that it blotted out the sun and blighted the land. I imagined it as a cross between a brontosaurus and a lizard with a tongue of fire, although my dad provided little in the way of physical detail. Maybe this was an old folk tale dating back to our African ancestors, or maybe it was an allegory for the racism that engulfed the South. I can't know for sure because my father knew only a small shard of the tale. Perhaps the

82   *The Graduate*

original got lost as it was passed down over the decades and through various family members until it finally reached me.

Another of Dad's tales was grounded in reality: the day his eight-year-old self gave his grandfather Seymour Simms a hot foot. I had never heard of this prank, but it's pretty much what it sounds like—lighting up a victim's foot with a match. Apparently, it was popular among baseball players. "Did you have any regrets about that, seeing as you loved him so much?" I asked.

"I thought it was so funny at the time, but it was cruel and could have really hurt him," he confessed. Until then, I had never seen my father sorry about anything he'd done. "I don't know why I did that to him. He was the only one who was always kind to me. I adored him. He was sick, you know, it even affected his speech. He never regained his strength from the fever he had."

Whenever he brought up Seymour Simms, he would mention the white people who called his grandfather "Cousin Seymour." "He was very fair skinned, and he was related to those white people," he said with a sense of wonder. Because most of the white people my father knew were so cruel, it was hard for him to comprehend this sign of recognition. One time, Seymour took my dad on a trip to Washington, DC. "He had relatives there—one of them worked for the post office," Dad said. At the time, this was a prestigious job for a Black person, and it would have marked this relative as a member of the city's Black middle class. "It was a world away from what I knew in La Plata," he said with a deep wistfulness.

Other stories were more sinister. "When I delivered the laundry for my grandmother, some of the white people would sic their dogs on me." (Like the Duke of Gloucester, despised by all: the "dogs bark at me as I halt by them.") Sometimes, he continued, "I would have to fight off the white boys in town. My grandmother told me to do whatever I needed to do to deliver the laundry because our family depended on that money. And I was afraid of her!" I imagined my father encircled by white toughs calling him foul names and trying to dirty the clean laundry he carried as he punched and kicked his way to safety. I had never been in a fistfight myself, but my dad's stories about the white townspeople of La Plata reminded me of what I had read in Malcolm X's autobiography or Richard Wright's biography. I had a throughline to all the Black history we were taught primarily during one month of the year, but my father's life *was* Black history.

Whenever my dad spoke about the white residents of La Plata, he also summoned the legend of presidential assassin and Confederate sympathizer John Wilkes Booth. He invariably described Booth as "a failed Shakespearean actor" from a family of some talent. As I later learned, John Wilkes Booth tried on for size the most iconic Shakespearean roles, including Macbeth, Mark Antony, and Richard III, his best-known role. But unlike his brother Edwin and his father Junius, he was unable to muster fully realized characters. The roles, like his name, were too large for him—which is why at the start of his career he called himself J. B. Wilkes, to avoid comparisons with his more successful kin. Yet despite his inebriation, his questionable talent, and his lack of elocution, Booth was a popular actor, largely because of his looks and his magnetism. He was famous for his daring stage leaps well before his last disastrous fall onto the stage of Ford's Theater as he shouted *Sic semper tyrannis* (thus always to tyrants) after slaying President Lincoln.[3] That phrase had already been incorporated into the Confederate battle hymn "Maryland, My Maryland," which became the official state song when my dad was fifteen years old (and remained so until 2021). The song refers to Lincoln as a despot and alludes to the movement of Union troops through Baltimore and the ensuing riot. Thus, my father's attachment to the legend of John Wilkes Booth made sense even beyond the Shakespearean connection, given that the La Plata of his youth was like a place preserved in amber—in many ways, it retained its antebellum flavor, especially for its Black residents. Descendants of the Confederates Booth attempted to avenge were responsible for preserving the Jim Crow social order.

My father continued his tale: "The Mudd family in Charles County were Dr. Samuel Mudd's people—the one who would treat Booth's broken leg once he fled the scene of the crime." The Mudds were one of the largest slave-owning families in the county, and Samuel served as a Confederate agent.[4] Coincidentally, my father's

84   *The Graduate*

name, John Samuel, was a combination of the names of two of the major players in this American tragedy. And there was another lesser-known player who also shared a family name: Mary Simms—a Black woman who was formerly enslaved by Samuel Mudd. As a newly freed person, she fled Mudd's household in 1864 after receiving a whipping from him.[5] Simms and other formerly enslaved people testified at Mudd's military trial. I don't think my dad knew about Mary Simms—who doesn't appear to be a relation—as I'm certain he would have remarked on her role in delivering the doctor's comeuppance.[6]

One of the Mudds my father was acquainted with was a lawyer. "He would sneak me into the courtroom so that I could hear oral arguments. I wanted to be a lawyer too," he said. I wondered about this white man who showed my father this small kindness. He may have been one of my grandmother's laundry clients and knew my dad from his delivery rounds. Or maybe this was a small act of expiation for his ancestor's betrayal of the so-called Great Emancipator and the formerly enslaved. In any case, it seemed he was not willing to crush the dreams of a young Black boy, although even that small transgression of the Jim Crow order was forbidden. To this day, the Mudds are a prolific family—they live all over Charles County, and several are practicing lawyers. But I have no way of knowing which branch of the Mudd family produced the lawyer who recognized my father's humanity.

Hell or High Water

I graduated from Sidwell despite my parents' financial troubles and the garnishment of my mother's wages. The latter was my fault. We were receiving so many calls about overdue bills that one day a collector badgered me and got me so flustered that I inadvertently tipped him off to my mother's second job. I was a horrible liar. I could tell my mother was disappointed with me, but she also knew she couldn't avoid the collectors forever. When my parents were late paying tuition my senior year of high school, Sidwell notified them that unless they paid in full prior to the graduation ceremony, I wouldn't receive my diploma, although I would be permitted to "walk" in my graduation ceremony. I had been a part of the Sidwell community since I was eight years old and had always been a stellar student, so this felt unnecessarily punitive.

I needn't have worried: there was no way my parents would deny me or themselves the satisfaction of a diploma. They were, after all, "come hell or high water" kind of people, so they did whatever they needed to do uncomplainingly. And both of them were strong believers in giving their children the best possible education, no matter the cost or the sacrifice. My dad in particular valued an academically rigorous education because he believed it would give his kids options he never had. In the end, they cobbled together the funds for tuition. My dad sold dinners on the weekends—my oldest sister cooked and I helped package orders; my parents pawned items of value (including my mom's diamond ring and some of my

86 *The Graduate*

dad's jewelry); and we borrowed the remainder from my maternal uncle. I worked that summer (and the summers thereafter) to save money for college.

The good news is that with my mother's documented jobs, she was able to fill out a Free Application for Federal Student Aid (FAFSA) so that I could get much-needed financial aid for college. This was impossible when Megan went to college because my parents' primary income back in 1988 still came from the numbers. My sister won close to a full academic ride to the University of Chicago, so she went there instead of her dream school, Columbia. I also won some scholarship money, and I was headed to the oldest Ivy League institution in the country: Harvard (which, ironically, was partially financed by a colonial-era lottery). I had never dreamed of going to Harvard until another Sidwell parent, a Black alumnus, intervened in my college application process and encouraged me to reach for the highest. Neither of my parents had attended college, and of my siblings, only Megan, Michael, and Carolyn had earned college degrees (Carolyn's coming later in life).

My admission to Harvard created a small controversy among a handful of Sidwellians. Although I was a top student taking three advanced-placement classes (biology, math, and art history) and had won a local journalism award for an op-ed I wrote for the school newspaper, there was some bitterness when my classmates learned I had earned early acceptance at Harvard. Of the four early applicants to Harvard, one was my *South Pacific* castmate Lieutenant Cable, one was a white female legacy, and two of us were African American. There were whispers about affirmative action from a person I had once considered a friend, even though in our yearbook's "In the Future, We Will See" section, my photo was captioned: "Johnisha graduate *summa cum laude*." My ex-friend's words bruised my feelings, but thanks to my parents, I was well aware of the hostile attitudes I would face—their own stories of racism and anti-Semitism were cautionary tales. I knew I would have to be much better than my peers so as not to be underestimated.

My dad holding me.

The day of my hospital homecoming, with my mother and my sister Megan.

(*above*): The day of my hospital homecoming, with my brother Charles.

(*left*): Visiting hours at Lorton. Left to right: my mother, my father, Megan, and Charles.

Visiting hours at Lorton. Left to right: my brother Adrin, Megan, my father, my mother (visibly pregnant with me), and Charles.

My dad displays his characteristic fashion sense at Christmas, as he and I sport matching grins.

(left) My father in his twenties after serving in the navy during World War II. It's the only photo I have of him from this era.

(below) My early days on Evarts Street NE.

(opposite, above) Left to right: me, Megan, my mother, and Charles outside our rollicking house in Northeast DC.

(opposite, below) Me playing the violin, around the time I learned "Missing You."

My father and me outside our house in Northwest DC.

My parents and me at the dinner table. Dad was a great cook, but even in the kitchen he wore his dress clothes.

My dad (second from right) and his associates looking like the Black Rat Pack.

My parents liked to go out on the town. Left to right: my mom's friend Alice, Mom, me, and Dad.

My parents and me at the Plaza Hotel in New York City, circa 1980s, when the street numbers operation was still prosperous.

My father and me. By the time I was in high school, my father was struggling financially, but he remained determined.

The Matthews family (kids, spouses, and grandkids) at my father's seventieth birthday party.

Close to the end of his life, my dad was impaired by dementia. (Photo by Charles Matthews)

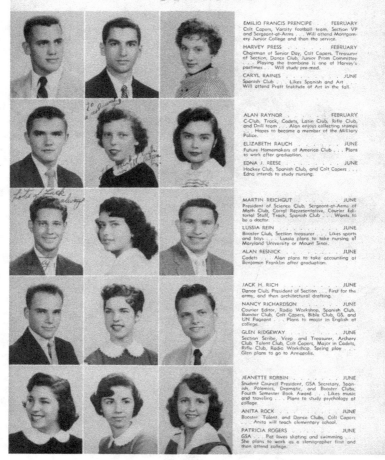

My mother's 1956 graduating class was very homogeneous, as this page from her yearbook shows. She's in the center of the third row.

My mother looks stunning at her first wedding, right out of high school.

I attended my parents' 1981 wedding.

The newly married couple.

My parents during one of their flirtatious moments.

Arlington Cemetery homegoing for my parents. (Photo by Charles Matthews)

Arlington Cemetery homegoing: presentation of the folded flag to my oldest sister. (Photo by Charles Matthews)

The Verdict

It was October 3, 1995, when the verdict in the O.J. Simpson trial was announced. I had been on the Harvard campus for only a month, so I was still figuring out how to coexist with the five young women who were my roommates. My mother and I had watched the TV coverage as the Los Angeles Police Department (LAPD) chased Simpson and his now iconic white Ford Bronco. Although I was not an avid watcher of the trial, I was aware of the highlights, including detective Mark Fuhrman's astonishing history of racism and attorney Johnnie Cochran's ploy to have O.J. try on the crime-scene gloves in front of the jury. ("If it doesn't fit, you must acquit.") I was in the Harvard Union having lunch with one of my roommates and a group of Black freshmen when we heard the news of O.J.'s acquittal. Many of us who attended elite private schools felt vastly outnumbered, misunderstood, and underrepresented, so we were relieved to find community at Harvard. Mealtime was a chance to relax, joke, and be ourselves, to lay down the unique burdens of attending a predominantly white institution. But on this particular day, all I felt was a sense of alienation and despair.

I watched with growing incredulity as one classmate beamed and high-fived another about the verdict: "He's free! He's free!" he exclaimed while muttering profanities about the LAPD. Intellectually, I could understand why they were celebrating the rare instance of a Black male defendant escaping the punishment of a racially biased criminal justice system. Emotionally, however, I couldn't forget that a woman's throat had been cut so deeply she had almost been decapitated, a young man had been slain, and two children had been left motherless and bereft. None of this was cause for celebration. I wanted to ask the celebrants if they had ever witnessed the life of someone they loved being choked out of them.

As I picked halfheartedly at the food on my lunch tray, I pictured my mother as a stand-in for Nicole Brown Simpson and imagined her fate if my father had drunk a little too much and squeezed a little too hard. The Simpson murder case made me reexamine my assumptions about the lines abusers would and would not cross during a domestic conflict. Years ago, my mom had told me that her first clue about my dad's temper was him kicking in the door of her shiny new Toyota when she was five minutes late picking him up. "I was thinking at the time," she said, "what is wrong with this man?" Yet this didn't cause enough concern for her to stay away from him. "Being the loyal person that I am, I stuck with him," she explained, as if she had read my next thought. "And that was the beginning of some very bad times," she deadpanned. Strangely, our mutual reaction was to laugh at this unvarnished appraisal.

Did we (my mother, myself, and broader society) lack the vocabulary to speak about domestic violence? I never asked her how the violence unfolded—whether it started gradually or arrived full force. Knowing my dad, it was likely the latter. The violence at home was ubiquitous; it was part of my earliest memories, so I took it for granted as an established fact of my life. I frequently worried about my mom now that I no longer lived at home. Although I was by no means capable of physically defending her, I was at least a dependable monitor of the abuse.

My mother was unequivocally the ballast in our household, but who did she have to turn to when my father's physical violence, verbal intimidation, and coercion became too much to take? "I told you to get off the damn phone," he'd bellow, intent on humiliating her whether she was speaking to her brother or a coworker. With equanimity, she would navigate the conversation until she could end it naturally, salvaging what was left of her dignity.

The Verdict 89

As a teenager, I frequently made the (ultimately futile) case for why she should leave him. "How can you stand it?" I asked, my voice inching higher in indignation. "Let's just leave!"

But even as my mother lamented my father's tyranny, she lauded him as "a good provider" for all his children. "I don't know if I can make it on my own," she said, citing her modest pay, which was already being garnished due to overdue bills that had gone into collection. Most confusing was her implication that my dad would disappear and not contribute to my upkeep if they separated, because in the next breath she would say with a sigh, "He's always wanted to do for his children." Then came the excuses: "He didn't have the right people in his life. If he had stayed with his own mother, he may have come out very different because Nanny was a kind woman."

The contradictions didn't add up for me. "But isn't a good provider more than a sense of material generosity or providing educational opportunity? Isn't it more than physical presence?" I'd fire back. Could a father like mine, who subtracts from his children's sense of security, dignity, and personhood, still be considered a good provider? Although my mother didn't recognize it, *she* was my good provider.

And what I didn't appreciate at the time is that my mother was trapped by generational and cultural expectations, as well as the inertia and fear that are common in victims of domestic violence. As Rachel Louise Snyder poignantly explains in *No Visible Bruises*: "We live in a culture in which we are told our children must have a father, that a relationship is the ultimate goal, that family is the bedrock of society, that it's better to stay and work out one's 'issues' in private than to leave and raise kids as a single mother. . . . The messages are insidious and they are consistent. We see those messages when our politicians wrangle over reauthorizing the Violence Against Women Act, and then fund it so sparingly it's practically a hiccup in the federal budget."[1] Add to this cultural messaging the reality that leaving is often the most dangerous time for abused spouses, and it makes sense why my mother held on. "They stay in abusive marriages because they understand what most of us

90   *The Graduate*

do not, something from the inside out, something that seems to defy logic: as dangerous as it is in their homes, it is almost always far more dangerous to leave. . . . Dangerousness spiked when a victim attempted to leave an abuser, and it stayed very high for three months, then dipped only slightly for the next nine months."[2] I also believe that my mother stayed with my father because she loved him deeply. I didn't understand it, but I could feel it.

Nicole Brown Simpson's fate was a sign of the cultural silence surrounding domestic issues—the wrongheaded notion that what happens inside one's home should remain there. This notion, which had been instilled in me since childhood, can kill. Thankfully, there is now greater awareness among the public health community. The Danger Assessment, created by domestic abuse researcher Jacquelyn Campbell, consists of twenty-two high-risk factors that predict homicide by an intimate domestic partner. Incidents involving strangulation are one risk factor: "Sixty percent of domestic violence victims are strangled at some point during the course of an abusive relationship—often repeatedly, over years. Those strangled to the point of losing consciousness are at their highest risk of dying in the first 24 to 48 hours after the incident from strokes, blood clots, or aspiration. Such incidents can cause brain injury— mild or traumatic—not only by cutting off oxygen to the brain, but because they are often accompanied by blunt force trauma to the head."[3] Every time my mother found herself in this situation with my dad, she inched closer and closer to dying, even without his use of a weapon such as a knife or a gun. Bare hands—my father's bare hands—were sufficient. While I was thankful she had lived through these encounters, I was ignorant of their cumulative and potentially fatal consequences.

Surprisingly, my dad had the occasional glimmer of self-awareness. When the 1993 Tina Turner biopic *What's Love Got to Do With It?* was released in the theaters, my father and I bought tickets for opening weekend. We were spending a lot of time together at the cinema in those days. I was bored because my mother was always at work, and with his senior citizen discount, he was a cheap date. Tina Turner was one of his favorite entertainers—he called her "my girl." But watching Tina (played by Angela Bassett) get beaten bloody by her husband Ike (played by Laurence Fishburne) with my dad was like an inmate watching *Shawshank Redemption* with his prison guard. I surreptitiously peeked over at my father in the darkened theater; he looked chastened during the climactic scene when Tina claims her freedom, leaving behind everything but her name. Instead of the hardened look he had when he abused my mother, I saw sorrow cloud his eyes, as if he were reliving painful moments from his own childhood. I was certain he knew that what he'd done to my mother—and to all his other domestic partners— was grievously wrong. But when we emerged from the theater, we both skirted the issue. I mumbled something like, "Poor Tina. She went through a lot." My dad nodded in silent agreement.

The O.J. verdict would remain in the back of my mind now that I had the freedom to try on relationships for the first time. Senior year of high school, I had thrown in the towel quickly—trying to navigate my father's temper was just too stressful for me. My would-be boyfriend—a harmless, slight brown boy who attended Sidwell— would have been the dream of most parents. But my father circled him like a predator as he carried out his interrogation. In fact, this boy looked a bit like Bambi as we left my house for the movies. In that moment, I detested my father, but I also hated it when people demonstrated their fear of him. I wanted someone to stand up to my father. I wanted *him* to be intimidated for once. The date was ruined before it even began, and my father's behavior ensured there wouldn't be a repeat.

In Massachusetts, I was far enough from home that my father didn't know everything I was doing. The boy I met and kissed at a party on the last day of freshman year would officially become my boyfriend during sophomore year. We were well matched when it came to relationship experience—both novices and virgins. He was the son of a union organizer and thus a fierce critic of American capitalism. He read everything from Adam Smith to Angela Davis and abhorred the two-party system. However, I would discover a glaring disconnect between his pro-feminist ideology and his

92   *The Graduate*

actions. When he got angry or frustrated with me, he told me to "stop acting like a bitch." He could be sweet and vulnerable, but also snappish and moody. I believed he was fundamentally a good and kind person who deserved some leeway, so mere words didn't drive me away. But my perspective changed one day in my dorm room. I was goofing around, trying to tickle him, but I had evidently missed the signs of his sour mood. "Cut it out!" he barked. I didn't, still giggling and oblivious until he wrenched one of my arms behind my back, forcing me to stop. "Hey, that hurts!" I yelled, on the verge of tears. "I was just joking around. What's your problem? Damn!"

That night, I kept replaying the scenario in my mind, asking myself how it was possible for someone to switch so quickly. Bending my arm back was minor compared to what I had witnessed between my parents, but it was a violation of my bodily autonomy, and it was unforgivable. I wasn't willing to entertain even the smallest possibility of replaying my parents' relationship. My boyfriend's action might have been a fluke or a momentary lapse, but I wasn't a gambler, especially not with my physical safety. I ended things immediately.

I met Dmitri when I stayed in Cambridge to take organic chemistry in summer school after my sophomore year. My friend G had invited me to hang out with Dmitri and another guy, a Bulgarian student who was dating one of my friends at the time. They were all part of the student cleaning crew, cleaning dorms to make extra money. The guys were playing pool in one of the dorms when I arrived. Dmitri had round cheeks and blemish-free, honey-toned skin a shade darker than mine. He was wearing a safari hat. Throughout the evening he was playful, even a little silly, but I liked that he didn't take himself too seriously. He seemed to lack the fragile ego of so many other Harvard boys I had encountered. He could throw barbs, but he could also take them in stride. I had the feeling he was going to be important in my life.

Later that night, as I headed back to my dorm room, I was unaware that the Bulgarian student had followed me. Within minutes, I heard a knock on the door. He told me he thought I had been sending him signals and asked to come in. I was astonished, especially given my friendship with his on-again, off-again girlfriend and his very public and explosive displays of possessiveness and jealousy. On one occasion, he lobbed a tray down the table of the dining hall, sending food and plates to the ground. Now, when I rebuffed him, his dark eyes flashed with anger. I worried that he might try to push his way into my room, but he opted to walk away without a fight.

The next time I ran into Dmitri I told him about the frightening encounter. His deep brown eyes were not smiling when he said, "Because I know him, I suspected something might happen. So I followed him to keep an eye on things. Had he not left, I was prepared to intervene."

Before long, I was smitten with Dmitri. As we talked, I marveled at how much we had in common. We were both the children of interracial marriage; our mothers were Eastern European, and we both strongly identified as Black. Dmitri spent his formative years in Ukraine with his tough-as-nails grandmother—a chemist and Communist Party member—who tried her best to shield him from Soviet racism. His nickname during those years was Chocolatka, but he was also called some other less endearing names. He was fluent in Russian, which wasn't much use when he returned to the United States shortly before college and found himself living in New York City's Washington Heights. There, he was mistaken by both the resident Dominicans and Puerto Ricans as one or the other, often causing uncomfortable misunderstandings. His explanation that he was a member of the other ethnic group in the neighborhood, Ukrainian, was not convincing. As a racial chameleon who was often asked either "What are you?" or "Where is your family from?" I could relate.

Given these commonalities, I wasn't too surprised when he shared a secret. One night that summer, we were hanging out in my sweltering dorm room, tying to keep cool with a fan that seemed more aspirational than functional. He had brought over a Peruvian CD, something to snack on, and a few candles. We were sitting at the small table in the corner of the front room I reserved for meals

94   *The Graduate*

and studying. Although Dmitri loved to joke around, we also had our share of heart-to-hearts. This time, he told me what happened to his parents when they arrived in the United States. The two of them had met in Ukraine when his Ghanaian father was attending medical school there.

"My father came here with the expectation that he would be practicing medicine, but the process was a lot more difficult than he anticipated. It was basically going to be impossible. He became disillusioned and desperate. He'd lie on the couch in the apartment. He'd start fights with my mother, and then he started to beat on her." His eyes glistened, but he maintained his composure.

"Oh wow." I faltered, unsure whether I should open up, but something told me it would be safe to finally share a secret I had carried inside for so long. "I know exactly what that's like," I admitted. "It's my life." Dmitri was the first person outside of my family that I told about the battering in my household. And he held it in confidence and poured more love into me. Finding someone who understood me and didn't judge me felt like a sign from the universe. He handled the dissolution of his own family with grace. He learned to fend for himself in Ukraine while his mother remained in the United States and subsequently remarried. I admired the fact that despite hardship, he exuded a sense of joy. Although he had only himself to depend on, he somehow managed to escape bitterness. I wasn't yet there, but I wanted to be.

In addition to experiencing a deep spiritual connection with Dmitri, I had finally found romance—someone who courted me, brought me flowers, wrote me notes, planned surprises for me, took me on real dates to restaurants. But it couldn't compensate for the man-sized hole in my life that could only be filled by paternal love.

I started to retreat from Dmitri emotionally. I was disconcerted by his unfamiliar combination of gentleness and strength. As much as I wanted to, I couldn't seem to accept a man in the role of nurturer. And so I began to mistake Dmitri's tenderness for weakness. It was as if my father's voice was in my head taunting me. When we were much younger, he called his daughters "dumb bunnies" when we failed to demonstrate a suitable amount of common sense.

That didn't really bother me, but lately he had started calling me ugly and laughing at the pain it caused me. "Little girl," he'd say, "if you don't toughen up, the world will eat you alive." He concluded with a mantra he adapted from the Danish prince: "I must be cruel to be kind."[4]

I became convinced that Dmitri loved me in a way I didn't deserve and could never reciprocate. My crushing guilt and regret made me distant and unkind. What we held in common and in confidence simply wasn't enough. A drunk Dmitri called me one night, professing his love. My father's internalized voice scoffed, "He's a crybaby. Wanh Wanh Wanh." Dmitri and I flirted with the idea of maintaining a friendship, but it just picked at the scabs of our prior relationship and was too much to endure. I had rejected him before he could reject me, and now I had to live with gnawing doubt: Would I ever be loved again? Was I even lovable at all?

Evidence of Things Not Seen

It all began with the book *May God Have Mercy on Your Soul*, a true-crime work that couldn't have been more remote from my own life circumstances. After college, I was working as a paralegal at a law firm and entertaining the idea of going to law school, but it wasn't until I picked up this book that I felt a sense of urgency about my future. The book covered the trial of Roger Keith Coleman, a white, blue-collar worker who had been convicted of the brutal rape and murder of his nineteen-year-old sister-in-law in Appalachian Virginia. What appalled me (and kept me reading) was the state's power to end a life, especially in light of the imbalance of resources between the government and the defendant. It may have been the possibility of Coleman's innocence that hooked me initially, but as I learned more about how racial and economic disparities determine who is charged with crimes and sentenced to death, I became wholeheartedly against capital punishment.

I moved forward with my plan and chose to attend New York University School of Law, where one of the preeminent advocates in the field of capital defense taught and trained the next generation of legal minds. I was not observantly religious myself, but it was obvious to me that Bryan Stevenson had committed his life to doing God's work.

Evidence of Things Not Seen 97

My father was ecstatic with my choice of career, which made me slightly uncomfortable—he was usually so stinting with his praise. "The baby's going to be a lawyer. A chip off the old block," he proclaimed to his friends, a wide grin spreading across his thinning and aging face. Simultaneously, my dad confronted his own crossroads. Although well past retirement age, he needed to find a new way to provide for himself and my mother. His three-decade career in the street numbers—which had paid for Catholic and private school tuition, family homes, modest vacations, and many of the other things enjoyed by middle-class families—was now vastly unprofitable due to legalization of the lottery in the District of Columbia (and around the country). Given my parents' desperate financial straits, my dad's advanced age, and his lack of an official employment record, he couldn't afford to be too selective. He readily accepted a job as a Salvation Army janitor, despite the grueling nature of the work, but it would be short-lived due to a heartless Christmastime staff layoff.

My father was not deterred. He learned through an adult education course catalog from the University of the District of Columbia that he could receive training and certification to be a home health care aide. He would be helping sick and disabled people with tasks such as getting out of bed, grooming, washing, changing clothes, and cooking meals. In some ways, it wasn't a completely crazy idea, as my dad displayed the most patience with his children when we were sick.

He had started writing me letters shortly after I left for college, and that is how I first heard about his new career path. It was sort of a rite of passage: as all his children became adults, my dad would put pen to paper and, in his spidery cursive, attempt to inspire or embolden us. If we talked on the phone, he had little to say beyond asking how my studying was going or commenting on the weather. But in his letters, he shared the things that lived inside his heart and that he was not equipped to say out loud. He seemed less self-assured and a little more transparent on paper than he was in person. "Your old man is going back to school to see what he can

98   *The Graduate*

make of himself," he wrote. "It has been a long time since I have been in any kind of classroom. I hope I don't embarrass myself."

"Dad, I'm so proud of you," I wrote back. "You didn't let things beat you. And you took a chance on something new. It's really brave!"

The summer before my senior year in college, I attended his graduation. His classmates—mostly elderly Black ladies wearing oversized eyeglasses attached to chains around their necks and red or pink Fashion Fair lipstick—flirted with him shamelessly. Women, after all, made up the majority of the home health care workforce, unlike the male-dominated world of the numbers. "Your father is so funny. Your father is so smart," they fluttered, as I tried not to roll my eyes. When I reported back to my mother, she dead-panned, "They can have him then."

He had dressed up for the occasion in one of his old (and now sagging) suits; he still carried himself with pride, but he wasn't quite the dapper dresser of yore. And for his new occupation there would be no need for sharply tailored clothes, even if he could have afforded them. All the home health care aides wore white uniforms.

My father also moonlighted a few nights a week on a cleaning crew, where he vacuumed and buffed the floors, took out the trash, and scrubbed the bathrooms in DC law firms. He was one of the only crew members who could converse with the lawyers, since most of the workers spoke little to no English. While he waited outside for my mom (and sometimes me) to pick him up at night, he would stand apart from the others, bundled up in a massive down coat on the coldest days. He would get in the car gingerly, a faraway look in his eyes as my mother drove off.

Law school was terrifying for a young woman who tended to get tongue-tied in front of authority figures (particularly male ones). I never got inured to the feeling of being put on blast in the class-room, where my mostly male professors battered my already low self-confidence. I developed a destructive habit of picking at my scalp during times of stress, to the point where I drew blood. But on the positive side, law school exposed me to passionate people

Evidence of Things Not Seen   99

filled with purpose and drive. Many of them wanted to better their communities and fight for the marginalized. I experienced a kinship with my classmates that had been largely absent in my prior schooling, and I began to follow politics for the first time.

Toward the end of my second year (2L, in law school parlance), I applied to work with Bryan Stevenson and the Equal Justice Initiative on behalf of indigent men convicted of capital murder. I had been energized during my 1L summer working at a nonprofit law firm in Chicago representing death row inmates pursuing state and federal appeals, as well as Illinois inmates applying for clemency. My bosses were a caustic older Jewish man whom I adored and a social worker turned attorney. They had chosen me as an intern because instead of just sending a letter, I had called to follow up about the opportunity. In Chicago, I lived in a crappy rental, which was all I could afford based on the meager scholarship NYU gave us for our unpaid summer work. The room had no air-conditioning, so I had to apply wet towels to my forehead at night until I was able to rent a window unit. On weekends, the bar next door blasted loud music, making it impossible to sleep. At least Megan (who had located my deluxe accommodations) lived in a neighboring suburb and could visit and check in on me.

During my 3L year, I moved to Montgomery, Alabama, for a full semester as part of the legal clinic's team of students. It was study abroad—social justice edition. Undoubtedly, I arrived in Alabama with some ingrained prejudices about the Deep South, gleaned from my avid reading and my father's experiences in the Jim Crow South. Some of these prejudices would be confirmed, but I would be disabused of many others. Sometimes when I looked at white Alabamans, I couldn't help but wonder whether their ancestors were pictured in those souvenir postcards I'd seen in books—the ones that made lynchings look like picnics, fun for the whole white supremacist family.

But what surprised me most about my time in the South was the openness of the people. Social niceties and courtesies that were in short supply in the Northeast were abundant there. When people asked you how your day was going, they really wanted to know. It

100 *The Graduate*

wasn't a perfunctory question meant to elicit an abrupt "good" or "fine" before moving on. And the people were genuinely helpful—if you needed directions or a hand carrying something, or if you just needed a pick-me-up, they were ready to respond.

Professor Stevenson taught us the etiquette of the region and the culture: how to express your religious ambivalence without alienating people ("I'm still searching for my church home") and even how to speak the language of the region's other religion—football ("Roll Tide"). To prepare for our work, we role-played how to have challenging conversations with families in unpredictable circumstances, while we crammed our heads full of the arcane postconviction legal procedure. After one of these simulations, Professor Stevenson complimented my ability to keep a neutral (nonjudgmental) face when my playacting family member shared information about her attempted suicide or the impact of incest. I remained calm and steady, displaying empathy but not registering the type of alarm that would have caused her to clam up. I thought to myself: at least my upbringing prepared me to keep my equanimity. Most important, the professor taught us how to carefully assess both the said and the unsaid, as well as our interview subjects' environment. No detail was too small, down to the interior of a house, and after every visit, we promptly memorialized our observations.

I studied Professor Stevenson closely because he was such an enigma to me. It was hard not to lionize him when the work he was doing was so incredibly important and, at the time, sometimes overlooked. Well before America heard of hashtags urging people to #SayTheirNames, before George Floyd died after enduring nine minutes and twenty-nine seconds of torture, before Breonna Taylor was shot in her home, and before presidential candidates tried to distance themselves from the 1994 Violent Crime Control and Law Enforcement Act (the so-called Clinton Crime Bill), Bryan Stevenson had not only created a network of attorneys to represent indigent defendants but also developed a legal strategy to change the nation's laws. (One of his most significant victories was the US Supreme Court decision banning mandatory sentences of life without parole for defendants younger than seventeen.) Yet in some ways he was surprisingly unassuming in a profession full of big egos and braggadocio. He was well groomed but not flashy. He favored shades of blue and black and classic ties, when he wore them. His hair was close-cropped to the point of being barely there, and his small shell-like ears were tucked close to his head. The cadence of his tenor voice reflected his Delaware roots—it was slower and more measured than the speech of New Yorkers but not as elongated as that of Alabamans. Every word was well chosen. You could tell when you had responded in a way that fell short of his high standards just by the way he held his head.

His sermon-like lectures always had a clear lesson he wanted to impart to his audience. He regaled us with tales of his grandmother's wisdom and of the injustices faced by his former clients. His grandmother, the daughter of an enslaved Virginian, would urge, "You can't understand most of the important things from a distance. You have to get close."[1] Professor Stevenson was also a jazz and classical music aficionado. He sometimes analyzed movie scores when he was talking to us about our work. He was of the opinion, for instance, that the *Million Dollar Baby* score didn't quite match the dramatic impact of the onscreen action. He adored the Bonnie Raitt cover of the John Prine song "Angel of Montgomery," which I had never heard before. It became our clinic theme song, and we knew who our angel was. But beyond his musical preferences, we could guess very little about his personal life. He seemed to live like a monk, cloistered in his cause with a group of talented acolytes. We mused in our free time what it would take to nominate him for a Nobel Prize.

We were divided into four teams of two students each, and each pair was assigned the case of one client. It was demanding work; most of our days were twelve to fifteen hours long, with a lot of time on the road between prison visits, family visits, juror interviews, and court errands. The work often continued deep into the night, whether in motel rooms or in the student apartment that was our home base in Montgomery. I spent hours reading and summarizing my client's lengthy trial record, keeping an eye out

102 *The Graduate*

for any deficiencies that might bolster an appeal based on the claim of ineffective counsel.

My client—I'll call him David—was thirty-four years old when I first met him at Alabama's Holman Correctional Facility. When my partner and I arrived at David's mother's house dressed in our black suits, she regarded us with deep suspicion. Because she didn't have a phone, she wasn't expecting us and assumed we were harbingers of bad news from the state. When we asked for her by name, she curled her lips and responded, "Who's looking?" However, once we explained who we were and why we were there, she proclaimed to the whole neighborhood, "These are David's lawyers!" No matter how many times we told her we were law *students*, she insisted on sticking to the lawyer label.

David was the Black son of a poor teenaged mother with a double-barreled Southern name. She had been schooled mostly in the cotton fields of Atmore, Alabama. As a migrant worker, she carried her young son to the snake-infested celery fields of Sanford, Florida. The figurative distance between her hand-to-mouth existence and the fantastical world of the newly opened Disney World dwarfed the fifty miles registered by an odometer.

> Drinking from mason jars, eating from pie pans
> Forks of trees cradling brown bags.[2]

David never did well in school. His IQ hovered in the high 70s, just above the standard for intellectual disability, but he knew what he needed to do to protect his loved ones. Initially, he was powerless when his mother's boyfriends abused her. His little-boy fists were no match for a grown man's. As he matured, he assumed more and more responsibility—much more than his tender years warranted.

> Ninth-grade man-of-the-house
> Acts to mother like a spouse
> New baby sleeps at the head of his bed
> Quits school to help sister-mom instead
> Sneaks into the yard sometimes to yell "hey" to friends.

Evidence of Things Not Seen   103

At sixteen, David met a girl and fell in love. The girl's mother loved David and offered him a chance to leave Alabama and find a better life in Lancaster, Pennsylvania. Though tempted, he decided that he couldn't abandon his mother, brother, and sister. They needed him. Shortly thereafter, the police started to harass David and accuse him of petty crimes. He and the girl eventually broke up, but her mother still cared about him and feared for his future in the small Alabama town.

David became a man and met a woman. He sold weed to help make ends meet, and the local police ramped up their pursuit. When the woman became pregnant, he wanted to celebrate his growing family, but money was short (as always) and Christmas was coming. That December, David either did or did not stab to death two white female convenience store clerks. Eyewitnesses were unreliable (one was a drug addict possibly motivated by the promise of a reward or the idea of revenge). The physical evidence was confounding: how did blood droplets from the gruesome murders end up only inside David's sleeve? His possibly coerced statement that he had been at the two convenience stores on the days in question, combined with the circumstantial evidence that he had paid his utility bills and purchased presents at Walmart, ultimately condemned him. He was convicted of two counts of capital murder and sentenced to death. The judge concluded with the customary words: "May God have mercy on your soul."

> Days and nights in dimmed out whites
> One hour a day of sunlight.
> Sister-mom copies words of God
> On cob-webbed sheets moist with sobs.
> Too sick, too broke, no wheels to visit
> Mutters son's name to those who listen.

The concept of mitigation in capital defense work is the theory that, as Bryan Stevenson puts it, "each of us is more than the worst thing that we've done."[3] When defense attorneys present mitigating evidence, it is with the hope that it will create a more nuanced,

104   *The Graduate*

holistic view of the crime and the defendant. It doesn't mean the defendant is "off the hook"; it only means that there are extenuating circumstances worthy of consideration.

In meeting David, I experienced neither fear nor hesitation; if anything, he was more anxious than I was. His body looked sinewy in his short-sleeved white prison uniform; he had a raw umber complexion and thick curly eyelashes. He was extremely solicitous, and in our subsequent meetings, he always asked whether the guards had harassed me and expressed concern about my safety during my extensive travels around the state to conduct the investigation into his case. He repeated himself a lot, probably because there was no one else to listen to him. For David, visits were a special occasion; he didn't get many because his mother lacked reliable transportation and lived sixty miles away. Plus, the years inside tend to add psychological distance between death row inmates and their families. David's main request, other than helping him win his freedom, was to get him a photograph of his six-year-old daughter, who had been an infant when he was first incarcerated.

At night, when I was alone with the so-called evidence of things not seen that I had amassed about David's life, I was reminded of my father's early life. But I hadn't expected that my investigation of David's case would provide a powerful new lens for probing a person's life history or that I would use it to reexamine my own family history.

David's story both was and was not my father's story. He too was a poor Southern Black son of a teenage mother who had to hustle to survive. Back then, I didn't know the circumstances of my dad's arrest and conviction, but now I am awed by the psychic pull that resulted in my counseling another incarcerated father and bringing him hope. Perhaps this link was wound into the helices of my DNA, something akin to intergenerational trauma. I knew some of the basic facts of my father's life through the stories he had told me, but in Alabama I felt their import and impact for the first time—how those circumstances shaped a young life in ways that were often vicious and unforgiving. Once the facts were given

Evidence of Things Not Seen 105

flesh and breath, they became painfully real. Professor Stevenson's grandmother was correct: "You have to get close."

And so it was that the apparition of a young John Samuel appeared before me. His head was almost perfectly egg shaped, his dark skin variably toned—the reddish hue of mahogany just along the nose, but shadowed under his deep-set eyes—his eyebrows so fine they were barely visible. He was long-limbed and lean, undernourished by the small game hunted by his family (possums, squirrels, and rabbits).

He was inquisitive and mischievous. Great intelligence radiated from his liquid black eyes. The most literate person in the family, his mother's oldest sibling, Aunt Belle, taught him the alphabet. When he eagerly carved out time to practice his reading, his twin uncles Joe and Ed taunted him mercilessly. They also terrorized him at his grandparents' home, waving a gun around and chasing him with it when they were drunk.

To escape, John Samuel found quiet kinship with his grandfather Seymour. Seymour would talk to him with loving patience. But Seymour's heart wasn't strong, he tired easily, and everyone knew that his wife, Lizzie, ruled the household. Lizzie's parents had been enslaved, and she had undoubtedly endured unspeakable horrors herself. She had been born right after the fleeting promise of Reconstruction had been broken by white men who wore sheets and rode at night. It was no wonder that she thought it safer to beat the promise, the ideals, and the dreams out of her young grandson—whipping him for the smallest offense—rather than have him end up swinging from a lynching tree like George Armwood.

At night, young John Samuel would look up and trace the constellations through a gap in the roof. After a tornado tore through the region, insurance companies refused to reimburse Black policyholders, so the hole remained.[4] He wondered, Why have I been abandoned by my parents? Why didn't they want me? Where do I belong? He couldn't fully comprehend the implications of his parents' youth and limited circumstances. He couldn't have known that Lizzie drove her daughter out of the house, scorned her, called her stupid, loose, and useless. So John Samuel was left to wonder:

was there more to life than grinding poverty, vicious racism, and the feeling that nobody really wanted you?

These questions would become more urgent when John Samuel's grandfather died three days after Christmas 1938.[5] Lizzie's second husband had no soft spot in his heart for John Samuel, who was growing into a handsome adolescent. He wanted no challengers in his small fiefdom, so he drove John Samuel out. But even when John Samuel moved to DC to live with his mother, he found that his days of fighting were far from over. His mother was demure and defenseless, and her boyfriends took advantage. One buried an ice pick in John Samuel's arm after he jumped into the middle of a dispute.

The world was savage, and John Samuel believed he had to mimic it to survive. He and a friend tried their hand at armed robbery, but he decided he wasn't cut out to be a gangster.[6] He did, however, have a talent for hustling; while working at the Government Printing Office, he started to loan people money. This was no doubt the beginning of his foray into betting and the numbers business.

And what of John Samuel's renewed relationship with his mother? She was a kind woman—an observant Catholic—but he couldn't forgive her for leaving him in La Plata. The two most important women in his life—his grandmother Lizzie and his mother—had hurt him deeply. He was willing to help provide for Nanny and defend her from others, but he also held on to a deep reservoir of rage. She had left him with Lizzie, and Lizzie had battered him. Now, all the future women in his life would be forced to pay for these crimes against him. He was especially vengeful when he drank; alcohol was fuel for his cruelty.

My father's first wife gave as good as she got both verbally and physically, but his subsequent wives and girlfriends cowered in the face of his violence. They would tremble and bend to his will, and often they would fold and break. As he connected with these women and then discarded them, he fathered more and more children, who became collateral damage. At first, the children were only stung by his cruel words and unpredictable temper; later, the boys were physically punished for both actual and imagined transgressions. Spare the rod and spoil the child, or so my dad believed.

These musings about my father revealed what happens to the soul under the duress of systemic racism, poverty, and societal and interpersonal violence. My whole life, I had watched my father beat my mother without ever really understanding where his anger originated. It had been easy to see him as the bogeyman haunting my waking hours. But now I could see two sides: my father as he was, but also who he might have been in a better, kinder world.

In some ways, little had changed in the decades between John Samuel and David. Many of David's family members and neighbors lived in dire poverty. Some of their trailer homes desperately needed repairs, and they lacked phone service. One visit revealed a person-sized hole in the middle of the trailer, which made me shudder out of concern for not only temperature control but also personal security. Contrast this scene with the storybook homes in Gulf Shores, a beach vacation community less than a thirty-minute drive away. Add to this the rigidly segregated neighborhoods and schools that never seemed to improve, despite the civil rights–engineered court battles. Could my father—or David—have made different or better choices? Maybe. But it is impossible to sit in judgment. What chance does an individual have against a system that is rigged against him? My father was a gambler throughout his life. He took what little he was given and turned it into more, although in some ways, it was not enough.

Ruminating on all this, I had an undeniable compulsion to dull the emotional pain these realizations provoked. The system and my family were broken, and I didn't know how to fix them. I felt powerless. Suddenly, I was forced to acknowledge who my father really was.

On the nights I conjured my father's past, I would physically stuff myself in an attempt to numb my feelings. I rapidly consumed a third of a box of cereal, a cup of peanut butter, or an entire sleeve of buttery Ritz crackers. My bingeing triggered a spectrum of emotions: the elation of fulfillment, followed by disbelief at my actions, and finally a lingering and excruciating shame that compelled me

108   *The Graduate*

to force the fullness back up. My shame was accompanied by a strident inner monologue—a voice so merciless that my father's cruelty paled in comparison: You are so pathetic. You will never be enough. Why do you even try? What is the point? You will never be pretty, successful, confident, or well-loved by one special person. I was unable to quiet the voice because it lived inside me. I believed everything this voice said, despite knowing that it derived its strength from the fact that it was inaudible to others. If that voice had been dragged into the open, I would have recognized its tyranny, and that would have shattered the power it had over me.

On my most despairing nights in Alabama, Marvin Gaye comforted me. Lately, Marvin had become my Shakespeare. I listened to his music over and over. His more upbeat songs such as "Hitch Hike" and "A Stubborn Kind of Fella" played in the car when my clinic partner and I drove the roads of southern Alabama, but when I was alone at night, I played his version of the spiritual "His Eye Is on the Sparrow." That song channeled all my heartache, my homesickness, and my grief. To this day, I cannot hear it without losing my composure. After the church organ intro, Marvin's vocals conjure all the pathos and longing of Black Americans. I imagine it is what sobbing would sound like if it could maintain melodic integrity and control. Forever stamped by the context of my time in Alabama, Marvin's "His Eye Is on the Sparrow" is connected to the sorrow I feel when I contemplate the childhoods of David and my father. In his interpretation, Marvin yearns for a second chance, for a better life, for a love that liberates. I'm not a prayerful kind of person, but listening to this recording is as close as I get to worshipping. I finally found my church home.

Graduation Day

I sought help for my eating disorder once I returned to New York City for my final semester of law school. But everything in New York seemed too raucous, too hurried, and too abrupt after spending three months exposed to the more deliberate rhythms and pace of the Deep South. I wanted to quarantine myself in my studio apartment and block out the noise. But of course, some noises, including my newly activated and abusive inner monologue, were impossible to suppress.

Even though I was attending therapy sessions, I was still acting in ways that were moderately to severely self-punishing. I avoided eating as much as possible, itemized my food intake in a small notebook, and limited my daily calories to a certain threshold I had set for myself. I used exercise as an additional means of weight control, keeping up the running habit I had started in Alabama. On "good" days, I would reward myself with something like a single low-calorie cookie. Otherwise, I would go to bed on the edge of hunger, which I found slightly euphoric.

My recovery would be neither quick nor easy. I needed to re-learn how to nourish myself. But the most important part of my treatment, which continued for years, was to reject the hypercritical inner voice and separate it from my innate self. Eventually, that voice spoke less frequently and grew weaker. Unfortunately, most of the people in my life were unable to come to terms with what I was doing to myself. Some of them pretended there was no problem;

110   *The Graduate*

others, such as my mom, blamed themselves. Healing from my eating disorder was one of the loneliest and bleakest periods of my life.

For this reason, it was helpful to have an important project to occupy my time when I returned to New York. Everyone in my law school class had to write a lengthy research paper—the equivalent of a thesis—to graduate. I waited until the last semester to write mine, in part because I knew my topic would be some aspect of capital punishment, and I wanted to see how my time in Alabama illuminated the issue for me. My paper was a comparative analysis of the antilynching crusade and the anti–death penalty movement, contrasting how Black voices were central advocates in the former but mostly victims in the latter. I wanted to propose ways to alter this discrepancy, so I buried myself in books, absorbing the words of African American crusaders such as Ida B. Wells, Mary Church Terrell, and Walter White, alongside theories of community activism.

On the day of my law school graduation, I hadn't regained any of the weight I had lost in Alabama, but I hadn't dropped any additional pounds either. I was holding steady, which was progress. My parents made the trip to New York City to attend my graduation, despite their still-tenuous financial situation. They stayed with me, sleeping on cots I obtained from my building manager. Johnny also drove up to help me transport my belongings back to DC in his SUV.

Graduation day started off as a proper celebration. I got little sleep the night before because I had stayed up late with some friends and was then kept awake by my dad's snoring. I slipped on a smart 1950s-style halter dress with a solid black top, white and black print skirt, and thin patent leather belt. My mom had found the dress at the department store where she worked. It had once fit perfectly, but it had to be altered to account for my significant weight loss. It showed off my long, slender arms and my hollow collarbones, which I thought were my best features at the time.

I tossed my formless black gown over the dress and grabbed my mortarboard, excited that I would be part of a contingent of Black graduates who were going to be "hooded" by critical race theory scholar Derrick Bell. Despite the somewhat problematic terminology (Black people generally try to avoid hoods), this symbolic gesture marks the passing of the torch from one generation to the next. The selection of a faculty member for one's hooding is therefore significant. Professor Stevenson would have been my first choice, but he was still in Alabama, shepherding the work of the Equal Justice Initiative. I hadn't actually had Professor Bell as an instructor. I probably could have worked out the scheduling conflict that prevented me from taking his class, but I was so irrationally afraid of the required long-form presentation that I cheated myself out of the opportunity to learn from him. I became acquainted with him when he graciously invited my small singing group, BALSA (Black Allied Law Students Association) Voices, to lunch at his favorite restaurant after we performed in one of his classes. That was when I worked up the courage to ask him about the hooding.

Backstage following the ceremony, my family presented me with a bouquet of red roses. My father was reveling in the moment as if it were his own. This made me happy, but I also had to suppress the urge to roll my eyes out of a sense of humility. In his own way, he was saying, "But yet thou art my flesh, my blood, my daughter."[1]

My mom looked smart in a white pantsuit and lapis-colored blouse. With her defined cheekbones and piercing green eyes, her new salt-and-pepper pixie hairdo was very alluring, and she had been getting a lot of compliments. I think this gave her a much-needed lift, especially as she was self-conscious about losing some teeth that she hadn't been able to afford to replace with a bridge. The hardship of the last several years had definitely aged her, and she no longer put much care into her appearance. Her department store uniform was some variation of black pants, black shirt, and black smock. At the deli, she wore my old T-shirts, including a spectacularly tie-dyed one I had acquired in sixth grade while on vacation at Rehoboth Beach.

My father was really feeling my mom's new look too. He gushed with praise, calling her "my love" and other mawkish things I hadn't heard before. Bleh, I thought, I don't need to see my father woo my mom after all this time. Even when my father was in a so-called good mood, he didn't act this way.

We all went out to dinner that night to celebrate: me, my parents, Megan, Johnny, and a good friend of mine. It had been a while since this particular family configuration had sat down together for a meal. Close by, I spied one of my best law school friends dining with her family, but I knew better than to suggest merging our tables, as an evening with my father was always unpredictable. This turned out to be the right instinct.

Megan had also invited a high school friend of hers to join us, but as soon as he arrived, the equilibrium shifted. Megan's friend was gangly, auburn haired, and white. He shouldn't have posed any sort of threat to my father, but he was diverting my mom's attention. Without any provocation, my father—fueled by Johnny Walker Black and jealousy—transitioned from a googly-eyed cornball to a jealous overlord. By this time, I had earned a doctorate in silent communication and picked up on the signs, but there was nothing I could do. His eyes narrowed, his grin disappeared, and he was starting to slur.

Thankfully, we made it through dinner without incident. But once we reached the sidewalk in front of the restaurant, ready to catch cabs back to our respective accommodations, my father let loose: "Hey, what's that FUCKING BUM want with my wife?" To my father, *bum* was the ultimate insult; it applied to those without morals, without conscience, without honor. It represented everything loathsome and disgusting; it was beneath human. Ronald Reagan (a "two-bit" actor and liar-in-chief), John Wayne (a racist and member of the John Birch Society), and George Wallace (the head racist) were all bums. Bums didn't have to be white, but they often were. "Hey, YOU BUM, I'll kick your ass!" my dad menaced. Then Johnny stepped forward and grabbed my father's arm, wrestling him away. "Calm down, Daddy, he isn't trying to talk to Lussia." This distracted my father and allowed my sister's friend to make an embarrassed and apologetic escape.

By the time my mother, my father, and I were in a taxi headed back to my building, I was shaking with anger. Within the span of a few minutes, my father had stolen the prize of my hard-earned achievement away from me. He had managed to burn up all the goodwill—and empathy—I had just started to accumulate for him, now that I better understood what he had lived through. I had prayed that just once he would behave himself, but he couldn't let us all enjoy a celebration without sabotaging it.

I suppressed my anger until we got back to my studio. Once inside, I looked at both my parents with contempt: "What the hell is wrong with you? Why did you have to ruin this one day? Why?" I included my mother in this tirade, even though it was 100 percent not her fault. But I had learned in therapy that I carried a lot of unexpressed resentment toward her, stemming from her failure to seriously consider leaving my father. She gave him chance after chance after chance. And now, after twenty-seven years of trying not to wake the volcano, all we had to show for it was the blistered and blackened soles of our singed tiptoeing feet.

The two of them looked at me, their eyes downcast, with the shame of scolded children. They knew there was nothing they could do to erase this memory from what should have been a joyous day. Any graduation photograph would now be a reminder of both how I had punished myself through my eating disorder and this moment of utter humiliation.

What I couldn't see at the time, because I was too close to the situation and entangled in my own struggles, is that this graduation would have been a triggering event for my father. He had every right to claim his child's success as his own, but perhaps my graduation was a bitter reminder of his own lack of achievement. His last child was moving forward with a career in the law, the career that he himself had once aspired to. He had already been abandoned by the world—forgotten as a child, supplanted as a numbers man, and replaced as a provider for his family. The final blow was to see himself, through a cloud of Scotch, usurped by this interloper who was "flirting" with his wife.

That evening, my brother and sister called and invited me to meet them at a bar for drinks. "Blow off the parents," Megan breezed. It was a classic Manhattan hotel bar, dark and hushed, with an adult ambience. I don't remember what I ordered because I didn't drink much in those days—the empty calories from alcohol were a waste. Instead of a fun, distracting evening, it turned into a badly enacted intervention. My siblings were worried about how thin I was and the stress I was putting myself under. They encouraged me to leave the parents to their own devices, as things were never going to change.

This immediately angered me. I would be living in DC after law school, and I needed to keep an eye on my parents, especially my mother. "This is *my* mom," I reminded my half-siblings. "I can't just walk away." I suspect this hit a bit of a nerve. Obviously we all recognized that my mom was their stepmom, but she had spent a good part of her life raising her stepchildren. I was bitterly disappointed that Johnny and Megan couldn't understand my perspective. They were older and had started their own families, so maybe they were better able to compartmentalize. But I was at a different place in my life, and I just couldn't. Their advice came off as blithe and out of touch. My mother had always been my protector, and I wouldn't stop being hers, even though I sometimes faulted her for her current predicament.

An Imperfect Mind

Fourscore and upward, not an hour more nor less.
And to deal plainly
I fear I am not in my perfect mind.

WILLIAM SHAKESPEARE, *KING LEAR*

My father's outburst at my graduation dinner was one of the last times I felt entitled to and justified in my anger toward him. Not long after, we began to notice evidence of a mental decline that would dramatically transform him into an altogether different person from the one I had always known. The first sign of this irrevocable change occurred in the summer of 2004. I had made the uneasy decision to take a job at a corporate law firm, starting in the fall. After my experiences in Alabama, I doubted I was resilient enough for capital defense work, and I couldn't ignore my family's financial situation. My three-figure salary would go a long way, even if I stayed for just a few years, toward taking care of myself, paying my debts, and helping my parents to the extent they weren't too proud to accept the assistance.

I splurged on a mother-daughter trip to New Mexico to celebrate both my graduation and my taking of the Virginia bar exam. We were in the airport returning to DC when my uncle called with a strange report about my father. "Lucy, John just called me," my uncle explained in his typically monotone voice. "He seemed really confused. He said something about the three of you were all on a bus, and that you and Johnisha told him to get off. And now he didn't know where you were or when you were coming back."

My mom and I tittered softly as we imagined a forlorn and helpless John Matthews stranded on the roadside with no way to get home. Most likely, we thought, he had dozed off and was just recounting a lifelike dream, although it was a little odd that he had called my uncle about it. We were sure everything would be back to normal once we got back to DC. And figuratively, we *had* left my dad on the side of the road so we could claim a sliver of time for ourselves.

The trip west was the reset I needed before starting my legal career. And my mother and I hadn't enjoyed a vacation in a very long time. For eight days, we relished being free of responsibilities and schedules. We drove with the car windows open and our hands hanging out. We stopped to take photos of the cerulean skies and the awe-inspiring Spanish and Indigenous architecture, including some of the real-life chapels captured in Georgia O'Keefe's paintings. Ever since I was a kid, these wistful moods had overcome me and I would say to my mom, "Let's run away." Her constant refrain was, "Where are we going?" to which I responded, "Away!" with a big sweep of my arms, as if that was an actual destination. This trip was the closest we got, and it would have been impossible with my father in tow. He didn't believe in meandering or just sitting and observing. It wasn't his style as a man of action. And although I had acquired his uptight attitude about punctuality, I was more than prepared to take things slow and easy on this vacation.

But in the months after we returned from New Mexico, we realized my uncle's phone call was more than just a fluke. What had started off as the ordinary forgetfulness of old age turned into both real and imagined losses of money, paranoia, forgetting everyday vocabulary, and maddening repetition.

During his decades in the numbers business, my father's brain had retained three-way combos and payoff odds like a human adding machine. When his livelihood crumbled, perhaps it was the final stressor that precipitated his dementia. Or perhaps his early exposure to racial trauma and childhood abuse accelerated his age-related decline.[1] The father who used to explain the Iran-Contra scandal to me in a way a third-grader could understand now stared for hours at the *Washington Post* as if attempting to absorb the printed words through osmosis, rarely turning the pages. He set kettles of water on the stove to make tea and then forgot about them until they had burned dry. One time, he stuffed himself into my mother's pants and never noticed they didn't fit.

And so my father remained bodily robust as his once-agile mind wasted away. He used more and more filler words, referring to "things" and "that woman" (my mom); called me by the wrong daughter's name; and resorted to discussing the weather as a default. I wrestled with a sense of overwhelming guilt because I much preferred this version of my dad—a gentle, quiet, adorable old man who could be easily managed. In fact, I sometimes disparaged my mom for "talking back" to him in a snappish way when he failed to comprehend instructions; then I recoiled with the realization that I had unwittingly become my father's defender. My mother repeatedly stated with conviction, in the voice of an Old Testament–style angel of vengeance, "God is punishing him by taking his mind away."

But was he being punished? I wasn't so sure. Deep down, I was conflicted about being cheated of my chance to meaningfully confront his misdeeds. Now that I was finally an adult and my own person, he was a meek old man who didn't know what day it was or whether he had eaten breakfast. How could I be livid at this shell of a person? How could I ever hope to hold him accountable for the pain he had caused? I realized that my father would never know how the years of his verbal and physical abuse had impacted his loved ones. There would be no resolution in this situation.

Despite my father's condition, my mother refused to consider putting him in a home any time soon. She was also certain that mayhem would ensue if she allowed strangers inside their home to care for him. She was fearful that even if she qualified for an at-home aide (despite my dad's status as a veteran, such expenses weren't covered), the person would steal from her. And one rare day when she took off work, she discovered that fresh-faced Mormon missionaries had been visiting my father for months and convinced

118   *The Graduate*

him to convert. She shooed them away with a scolding: "He doesn't know what you're asking of him! He's been a Catholic all his life." Finally, it was a point of pride for Mom to take care of Dad at home, just as he had considered it his responsibility to provide for the household. As always, my parents kept their problems to themselves.

And for years, the arrangement more or less worked. He listened to my mom and was no longer violent. Most days, he would sit peacefully with their dog Maggie at his feet or on his lap. He was able to take her for short walks without getting lost or confused. He retreated to the past, back to a time he could more readily recall. He had developed a script, for instance, when it came to relating World War II anecdotes. "You had to watch out for those coconuts, because their velocity as they fell could be fatal," he repeated over and over while my mom rolled her eyes. He started to assist my mother with cleaning chores around the house ("I'm working my fingers to the bone," he'd chuckle). And he even ate pizza, the sight of which had previously triggered a condescending, "You call that food?" Miraculously, his sharp wit remained intact, and on good days he could fool a visitor into thinking he knew what was going on.

Much of the news about my father was now filtered through my mother because I no longer lived in DC. I had moved away in stages. The year I started at the law firm, I leased my first apartment in Northwest DC, about a fifteen-minute drive from my parents' house. Next, I relocated across the bridge to Arlington, Virginia. My biggest and boldest move was to the Boston area. I had finally taken my siblings' advice, not because I was fleeing responsibility but because I was living my own life. And yet I couldn't leave behind my wrath or my confusion about these irreconcilable versions of my father.

On December 10, 2012, my mom returned home from her retail job, weary and footsore. She collapsed on the living room couch with the dog by her feet. She watched as my father left the house attired in a puffy red vest, dark corduroy pants, and a baseball cap. In his later years, he had started wearing softer, looser-fitting clothing my mother bought him, reflective of his new mental state.

Over the years, my father had walked out the front door of 1439 Oglethorpe many times and in many ways—sometimes purposefully, sometimes vengefully, and lately blankly and instinctually. When he hadn't returned in a reasonable amount of time, my mother got worried. She jumped into her blue 2005 Toyota Corolla, its front passenger seat covered in tufts of Maggie's black fur, and rode up and down the streets of her 16th Street and Georgia Avenue neighborhood, looking for my father. After hours of futile searching, she returned to the house alone. She didn't get a bit of sleep, yet she waited another twenty-four hours before alerting the family that my father was missing.

She finally reported his disappearance to the Metropolitan Police Department, and they issued a silver alert for a missing senior. She called me in Boston to let me know. "What do you mean, missing?" I asked. "How long has he been gone?" It didn't seem real to me. It was like the plot of an old movie where the father goes out for cigarettes and never comes back, but with much darker overtones because of what could happen to an eighty-eight-year-old man with dementia on the city streets. Had he been robbed, beaten, shot, or worse? My mind rotated like an old slide projector through all the horrid fates he might have suffered. The only thing my husband and I could do was drive down to DC, rather than fly, so we would have a car and be able to scan the city for my father or for any clues that might lead to him.

The search was a complex effort on multiple fronts. In addition to alerting the police, we combed the frigid city streets distributing printed flyers featuring my dad's picture and description. My family and friends checked hospitals, homeless shelters, barbershops, and even the corner store where he liked to buy his Mr. Goodbars. We scoured the portion of Rock Creek Park off Kennedy Street, where my father sometimes walked by the Carter Barron Amphitheatre. We knocked on neighbors' doors and followed up on every clue. A lot of people recognized my dad from the neighborhood and mistakenly thought they might have seen him around. A barber told my brother and me that maybe my father just didn't want to be found. I wanted to yell at him, "Dude, he's eighty-eight years

120   *The Graduate*

old, where would he be going in his right mind?!" Instead, I bit my tongue. "Just let me know if you see him around," I said with an uncharacteristic iciness as I handed him a flyer. One night, a homeless woman swore she had seen my father downtown, in line for a mobile meals service, and she pressed my crying mother's hand to offer comfort.

None of these leads took us anywhere closer to finding my father. Eventually, my husband and I had to return to Boston, leaving my brothers to continue the hunt for my dad. There would be no long good-bye, no final illness in hospital or hospice, and no last breaths to sob over. The sound of the front door shutting would be my father's final exit from our family.

Four weeks later, a woman walking her dog near the part of Rock Creek Park proximate to Silver Spring, Maryland, discovered the body of an elderly Black man. This was no more than three miles from my parents' house, but in the opposite direction from where we had concentrated our search. My mom and one of my brothers had to identify the body. In the meantime, a reporter at the *Washington Post* had leaked the story to a law school colleague of mine, who sent me a text message to extend her condolences. This lapse of ethics incensed and stunned me more than the sentiment comforted me. We had no time to process my father's death in privacy. Since we didn't know the actual date my father passed away, we commemorated it as January 7, 2013, the date his body was discovered.

My mother asked me to pen an obituary for the funeral program my brother Charles was putting together. He went way beyond cheap paper and fuzzy black-and-white photos, using glossy colored paper with overlaid text on photos and insets. Charles also designed and printed beautiful photo collages to display on easels around St. Augustine's during the service.

I had conflicted feelings about my father's behavior, but my mother knew I would be able to tell a compact and empathetic life story for a general audience. I sat down at my laptop to pound out an abbreviated version of a long life spent mostly in DC and always close to his family. It wasn't difficult to compose the four paragraphs—a strange calculus when you think of it as each paragraph covering more than twenty years. I attempted to pay homage to his drive and his intentions:

> His hunger for knowledge transcended the limited opportunities that segregation afforded him. He loved poetry, recitation, and reading and dreamed of becoming a lawyer.
>
> After graduating as valedictorian of Bel Alton High School, he moved to Washington, DC. He was later drafted into the United States Navy. He served valiantly as a radioman in the South West Pacific theater (the Philippines, Borneo, and Papua New Guinea). His service was transformative in many ways. He experienced the stings of segregation, but also made unlikely friends and allies. He learned about other cultures.
>
> He was a strong believer in education, and encouraged his children to seize opportunities in this avenue that he himself was not afforded. He valued their achievements as his achievements.
>
> In later years as his Alzheimer's progressed, he lived a quiet life. He found constant companionship in his pet dog, Maggie.

Once the desperate drama of his disappearance subsided and the emotional memorial service was over, I was surprised by how clear-eyed and pragmatic I felt about my father's passing. After a loved one's death, we often hold them more gently, lest we break them in our memories, or we dim their defects and magnify their virtues. But in the days, months, and years that followed my father's death, I experienced more than anything an absence of feeling. My voice didn't catch when I spoke about him; I was steely and callous, just as he wished me to be. As old King Lear said to his youngest daughter Cordelia after she refused to falsely flatter him, "Nothing will come of nothing." I suspect my father was very tired of being trapped by his imperfect mind. "They oughta take them out and shoot them": that was how he talked about his elderly peers who had lost their purpose, common sense, bodily health, or all three.

122   *The Graduate*

Perhaps he looked in the mirror and saw "a poor, infirm, weak and despised old man," and in a moment of lucidity, he could no longer bear it.[2] Maybe he left the house intending to direct his own demise; maybe he didn't get lost at all but just lost all of us. Either way, he was irrevocably lost to me after I had spent my whole life trying to discover who he really was.

And so, I was left to wonder whether I would ever make peace with my father. Something had always held me back, despite my evolving view of human nature. And yet, there was one more surprise awaiting me as part of my posthumous investigation of his arrest and incarceration. This time, it related to my mother and how she succeeded in keeping our family together despite the long odds.

Part 3
THE GUARDIAN

Basic Human Needs

I impatiently scrolled through the scanned document on my cell phone. After picking up the lawyer's files pertaining to my father's case, my friend Nicole had emailed whatever she thought I would want to see right away. This document, sent by my mom's attorney to the prosecuting assistant US attorney, was included. Nicole had warned me to wait until I ended my workday before looking at it, but I couldn't stop myself. It read:

> Ms. Rein received a probationary sentence from Judge Flannery in 1977, when John Matthews, the father-to-be of the child she was carrying went to Lorton. Ms. Rein was without the ability to work at regular employment because of severe difficulties in her pregnancy. She was in substantial need of funds for medical treatments, having already suffered numerous miscarriages in the past. Determined to bring this child to full term and attempting to support other children of Mr. Matthews, she acted as a clerk and manager for his numbers business for approximately two and one-half months. She was then subject of a search by the FBI at 1545 18th Street. What she did during this two and one-half month period was against the law. But it was also the product of basic human needs that could not otherwise be fulfilled. Ms. Rein has but one conviction . . . I do not believe it would serve any community interest in these

circumstances for Ms. Rein to leave her 10-month-old child and be incarcerated as a result of the events of early 1977.

I instantly regretted my decision. As I read the letter and the subsequent order issued by the Superior Court of the District of Columbia, my sight blurred. I was still working from home due to the pandemic. My head was throbbing and my heart was vibrating wildly, so I withdrew to my bedroom and remained there for hours, hiding within the cocoon of my duvet. Every time I attempted to regain my composure, I dissolved. It was the most visceral pain I had experienced since my mother died of cancer in 2015. It was like grieving her all over again. How close I had been to losing her before I even knew her! I kept thinking about how much more I would have suffered without her protection and her nurturing. If I had been robbed of the great love in, and of, my life, it would have changed everything. To understand that all three of our fates—my father's, my mother's, and mine—were in the hands of a court was chastening.

Eventually, I pulled it together and texted Nicole: "I keep thinking what if they hadn't had a good lawyer? Or what if my mom had been Black? Chances are she would have been sent to prison too. Then I could have been in foster care or in some other horrible position." I shared the same thought with my husband, Jon, who (thankfully) is much more of a glass-half-full kind of person than I am. "I understand that," he said, "but instead of dwelling on what might have happened, think about how your parents did everything in their power to prevent that worst-case scenario. It's incredible!"

But Nicole's response validated the highly emotional toll of coming face-to-face with the closest of calls, as well as the innate bias of our criminal justice system: "I thought that very thing driving home," she texted. "If your mom was Black, the outcome would have been very different. J, you were her miracle baby in more ways than one. I kept thinking about your mom holding it all together with an infant and the older kids with all of this hanging over her head for 18 months!" It is something I cannot begin to imagine, even though I have now passed the age my mother was when she had me and married my father, in that order.

For my entire life, I had seen my mother "through a glass darkly." Our relationship was complex, but we were always friends. I often preferred to hang out with her rather than my high school friends. We would get burgers at Chadwick's, across the street from the department store where she worked, and she would share the latest drama surrounding her colleagues. Or we would order a rectangular pizza at Ledo's and discuss my latest hopeless crush. She was also my fiercest protector—anyone who messed with me had a sworn enemy. ("I'm not afraid of the death penalty," my mother quipped when the guys I dated didn't meet with her approval.) And we never had those knock-down, drag-out fights that other mothers and daughters have, like she and Megan sometimes had. Of course, we were also fellow hostages being terrorized by my dad. Yet an essential part of my mother was entirely obscured from me, a part that she actively hid to give me a sense of normalcy—to give me the easy and untroubled origin story she thought I deserved.

"I do not believe it would serve any community interest in these circumstances for Ms. Rein to leave her 10-month-old child." For the next couple of weeks, those words were tattooed on the inside of my eyelids. I never expected to read about my infant self in legal files, let alone discover that my mother had jeopardized her freedom by getting involved in the numbers game not once but twice. I never imagined that a court had the power to sever my most vital relationship.

I was aware of only the vaguest outlines of my mother's participation in the numbers business, but I knew there was more to the story. When I was a teenager, while talking to Megan during one of her visits home from college, I mentioned memories of Mom bringing me along to do community service. Megan blurted out the truth, no doubt relishing having the upper hand over her little sister. "Well, yeah," Megan said. "That was part of her probation."

"Her probation for what?" I asked innocently.

"Well, you know she was involved in the numbers too. With Dad. I mean, she wasn't doing community service just because she was a nice person," she scoffed.

After Megan's revelation, I never asked my mother about the nature and extent of her involvement. I figured she had her reasons for withholding that part of the story.

It is now apparent that I was the impetus for my mother's early "retirement" from "the business." She didn't want to risk a third strike, as that probably would have led to a prison sentence. She didn't want to abandon me after waiting so long to have a child of her own. Now that she was gone, I had no reason not to piece together as much of the truth as I could.

Probation

Once again I started with my brother Johnny, hoping he could fill in some of these new blanks. And he did have some answers. My mother had started off as a bagman for my father, delivering payoffs to the lucky winners. It was an unlikely sight: imagine a breathtaking woman in a Pucci print dress and Bruno Magli shoes distributing money to street bettors. Johnny put it even more bluntly: "Lussia was a showstopper, man," shaking his head in emphasis. "I mean, my friends would say to me, 'Who is that? That's your dad's girlfriend?' It was kind of embarrassing for a teenage boy because, you know, you have lots of feelings then."

My mother would have drawn attention for other reasons—she was a younger white woman working in an underground operation run by mostly older Black men and a few older Black women such as Odessa Madre. My dad's reputation on the street would have offered protection as my mother transported large sums of cash across the city (no one wanted to get on the bad side of Johnny Matthews), but it wasn't completely foolproof. I recall a story she shared in her later years that I could now put into context, knowing that she had been fully entrenched in the numbers operation. She had been held up at gunpoint in the stairwell of an apartment building. "Your dad said, if anyone ever robs you, don't try anything. Just give up the money. So I did, and luckily that was all they wanted and let me go." In retrospect, it made sense why she kept a wooden stick slightly smaller than a baseball bat in our car.

As I reviewed the relevant court filings, I discovered that my mother had not been charged in the same case as my dad. The FBI had started investigating her codefendants, several members of the Lincoln clan, as early as 1969 because they were allegedly running "one of the largest gambling organizations in the Washington, DC area." Ollie Lincoln had assumed control of the numbers business following the death of Whitetop Simpkins, an old-time numbers operator and community philanthropist. Simpkins was so well known and respected that "when the D.C. Council was discussing legalizing the numbers game rather than instituting a government-run lottery, former chairman John Hechinger said, 'We might want to get Whitetop Simkins to design it for us.'"[1]

I'll never know the nature of the relationship between the Lincolns and my parents and why my mother worked for them. This investigation, like the one that had netted my father, utilized the full spectrum of law enforcement tools: confidential informants, pen registers, and wiretaps. Ultimately, as a result of this surveillance and seizure of evidence, my mom was indicted in January 1975 for making two unlawful "telephone communications in connection with illegal gambling." This was minor stuff, but it had consequences. As in my father's case, attempts to suppress the wiretap evidence were unsuccessful, and my mom was sentenced to three years' probation in March 1976. By the end of 1976, she was pregnant with me.

By early 1977, my father was headed to Lorton Correctional Complex to serve his time. My mother would have discovered she was pregnant after my father was already inside. In some ways, the timing couldn't have been worse, but my mother desperately wanted a child of her own, and given that she was thirty-nine at the time, this was likely her last chance.

With my father gone, she was also left to care for four of his underage children who were living at the house on Evarts Street. Faced with the weighty question of how to keep the household running financially, my mother chose to carry on my father's business. Although he had some loyal lieutenants, he was no doubt anxious

Probation 131

about how his absence would affect his business. My parents probably had coded discussions about the numbers operation and how to manage it when my mother visited him in Lorton.

When I confronted Johnny with the information I had gleaned from the court filing, he was unfazed. "She knew all the contacts, everything," Johnny told me. "It was impressive." He was sixteen at the time, so he overheard a lot of conversations and understood their import much better than seven-year-old Megan did. I recalled my mom's interactions with all the folks in my dad's U Street orbit—how comfortable she was conversing with them. Now I knew it was because they had worked together. But I had noticed this sense of familiarity even when I was a little girl, accompanying my mother to pick up my father from "work." It was even more apparent when my father disappeared and we walked his old stomping grounds, hoping to retrace his steps. My mother was utterly undaunted when strange (to me) old men approached us. She introduced me, and I listened as they shared memories or talked about people they had both known who had fallen on hard times or passed away. She was part of the numbers universe.

Despite the precautions she no doubt took when operating the business during my father's absence, she was ultimately apprehended—again. The DC Gambling Squad remained focused on street numbers in the lead-up to the launch of the DC Lottery in 1980. In April 1977, four months before I was born, the police searched an apartment at 209 18th Street, a residence my father maintained, where he had once lived with Megan and her mother. My mom was arrested as a result of the evidence gathered. Her attorney, the same one my father used in his appeals, pleaded her case as a mother who did whatever she needed to do to survive.

I can imagine how terrified my mother must have been at the thought of losing me because I knew she had miscarried numerous times. She most often mentioned a son, born during her first marriage, who had lived for only a matter of hours. "I fell apart," she explained tearfully. "It was the hardest thing that had happened to me." I knew what that meant, given that she had lost both her little brother, due to a congenital heart defect (she found him dead in his crib), and her father by the time she was fourteen—the same age my father had been when he lost his grandfather Seymour Simms. She spoke glowingly of her father and her memories of him. "He was a soft-spoken man, gentle. He was very talented and could make anything because he was a furrier. He sewed my little dance costumes and some of my dresses," she said, pointing out her six- or seven-year-old self wearing a little floral tunic in a small black-and-white photo with crenulated edges.

After a string of miscarriages, my mother's obstetrician-gynecologist diagnosed her with an "incompetent" cervix, meaning that it opened too early, making her unable to carry to term. "It was Dr. Stewart who enabled me to have a normal pregnancy. He was this really sweet man from Minnesota, I think he was of Scandinavian ancestry. Sterling Stewart. He is the reason for you," she told me lovingly. The medical procedure mentioned in the court papers was likely a cervical cerclage, wherein the cervix is sutured to keep it from opening prematurely. Now I had even more information about the stress my mother had endured during her pregnancy.

In light of her lawyer's letter, the court delayed my mom's sentencing until December 8, 1978, to explore the options. Ultimately, she was allowed to remain on probation, provided she refrained from committing additional crimes, completed a number of hours of community service, and agreed to reasonable discretionary searches. Thus, I was rescued from an uncertain future and perhaps the custody of strangers.

Spirits in the Material World

My mother is often missing from my infant and toddler photographs because she was the one holding the camera. In one photograph in which she does appear, she looks like a stunning 1970s-era Madonna with child. I am about a year old and newly walking. It is clearly summer because I am wearing nothing but a diaper and a mint green T-shirt. I have started to lose some of my roly-poly Buddha baby fat, but I still have small pinchable rolls. My mother is wearing a sleeveless flowered sundress in shades of blue with purple and yellow accents; her long dark hair is tied back in a ponytail. She has the hint of a smile on her face, and her arms are outstretched as she bends to guide my tiny shoulders toward a white stone flowerpot containing a bright red geranium. She will not let me fall.

To me, this photo captures my mother's quiet confidence that someone or something was always watching over us, some spiritual or ancestral power. Whenever I came to her with my worries, anticipating the worst-case scenario, she would tell me, "Things have a way of working themselves out. Cross that bridge when you get to it." And she was usually right. Simultaneously and perhaps contradictorily, she had a dramatically dark vision of the world as being full of people with sinister motives. Faith and fear—those were the two polestars of her existence. She did not trust in the good side of human nature, especially when it came to the most vulnerable human beings: children. She warned me about child molesters before I could even properly pronounce the word (prior to speech therapy, I called them child moblesters) or understand that they did more than just abduct children.

Instead, my mother trusted her own intuition, which was so finely tuned that she frequently experienced premonitions. "I'm a witch," she would playfully claim. "When I think of someone, they call or show up." And it was true. She would mention some random person, such as one of her coworkers from decades ago, and out of the blue, that person would call. Or she would dream about my paternal grandmother wearing black, and some illness or other misfortune would befall someone close to us. She also claimed to see and feel spirits—her deceased mother, Sylvia, tapping her on the shoulder while she tended her roses and peonies, or Sylvia sending a sign by making the lilac tree bloom in a shower of delicate buds after years of dormant, bare branches.

My mother taught me that the antidote for the evil eye (essentially a concentrated form of envy directed at a person's good fortune) is to say the Jewish word *kinehora* while spitting three times over the shoulder (in case the word alone did not suffice). She warned me not to cut my toenails and fingernails on the same day because that is the Jewish ritual for preparing dead bodies. She admonished me not to let anyone step over me, for it would stunt my growth.

My childhood was vastly different from the rigidly Catholic upbringing of my brothers and sisters. Although I never attended Hebrew school or synagogue regularly, I imbibed all the folk culture of Old World European Jewry, along with seven years of Catholic mass and communion. But when I changed schools, and as my father became more disillusioned with Catholic dogma (especially with regard to divorce), I absorbed more and more of my mom's cultural Judaism. This was natural, given that she was the person I felt closest to, and her own family was so diminished. She always told me, "If a mother is Jewish, so is her child," so I began to identify as Jewish as well as Black.

Spirits in the Material World 135

My mother's conception of the world was undoubtedly driven by her grandparents' Orthodox beliefs, her coming-of-age during the war against Nazi Germany, and the Old Testament God—a God who was alternately vengeful and vain yet loyal upon demonstrated fealty and therefore much more human (and flawed). This God didn't turn the other cheek, and he could be relentlessly cruel, but he did not abandon his chosen people. This was analogous to the shadowy, dangerous world she and I inhabited alongside my father.

All the same, I demonstrated an early skepticism about my mother's faith. One day, we were at the mall, and she was trying to lift both three-year-old me and my stroller onto the escalator. Somehow, she cut her ankle, and I looked down to see drops of blood blooming like a bright scarlet poppy beneath her pantyhose.

"Thank goodness, God was with us," she said with relief.

"I didn't see God, Mom," I responded. "It was just me and you."

Two Weddings

Often did [I] beguile her of her tears
When I did speak of some distressful stroke
That my youth suffered. My story being done,
She gave me for my pains a world of sighs.
She loved me for the dangers I had passed
And I loved her that she did pity them.

WILLIAM SHAKESPEARE, *OTHELLO*

From the outside, the wedding was a fairy tale, complete with a beautiful Snow White princess—flawless pale skin, raven hair pinned up to frame her perfectly symmetrical face, and an exquisite gown.[1] The bride, who was Ashkenazi Jewish, had the exotic beauty of racially ambiguous Hollywood actresses such as Merle Oberon and Lena Horne. The groom wasn't quite princely (though he was neat and stylish), but the bride's perfection compensated for his ordinariness. They were contemporaries in age and similarly small in stature. They signed a *ketubah*, an illustrated Jewish marriage contract that obligated them to each other. The bride "plighted her troth unto [the bridegroom], in affection and in sincerity, and has thus taken upon herself the fulfillment of all the duties incumbent upon a Jewish wife." The date of the wedding, in the Hebrew calendar, was the sixteenth day of Kislev in the year 5718, which corresponded to December 8, 1957. (Coincidentally, the bride would die on the same date fifty-eight years later.)

136

The groom was not my father but my mother's first husband, Alvin. Alvin remained devoted to and besotted with my mother even after their divorce, so much so that he intervened in mysterious ways to save my parents' house when they were on the verge of losing it. But my mother was never in love with her first husband. Rather, my grandmother Sylvia had convinced her that getting married was the "right thing" to do. Sylvia, a new American who had fled the anti-Semitism of interwar Europe, was in an economically precarious position as a widow and the sole support of her household. She was an Orthodox Jew from Eastern Europe, with its strict conceptions of gender roles. Sylvia frequently quipped that her father had four boys and two slaves, the latter being the girls in the family. She never encouraged my mother's dream of attending nursing school.

My mother's first marriage came to an end after roughly seven years, while she was in a fog of grief over the death of a baby boy who had lived for just a few hours. "I was just so heartbroken, I needed to walk away. I had nothing else to give," my mother explained years later as she fought back tears.

Her second wedding—to my father—took place more than two decades after the first, in 1981. It was anything but conventional. She was forty-two; my father, fifty-six. Both were divorced. And they were among the first generation of interracial couples who got married following the 1967 Supreme Court ruling in *Loving v. Virginia*, which banned antimiscegenation laws in the United States.

Certainly, the union of my white mother and my Black father made them a rarity for the time and place, but they would have turned heads anyway: they were a physically striking couple. This wasn't merely my opinion. Whenever I shared photos of them or when my parents were out and about, inevitably someone would remark, "Your mother is so stunning. Your father is so charming."

For her second wedding, my mother wore a two-piece pink skirt set, her shoulder-length hair curled at the ends with hot rollers. (As a youngster, hot rollers fascinated me. I would watch excitedly as Mom plugged them in and added the water, which began to hiss and steam.) My father, with his upright posture and Habesha good

138   *The Guardian*

looks, was dressed in a dark three-piece suit that restrained his prosperous-looking paunch.[2] The white priest who presided over the ceremony was a longtime family friend who sported a '70s style shaggy mustache, long sideburns, and large glasses. Most of my father's other children were in attendance, along with three-year-old me. I wore a fluffy Jewfro, white patent leather shoes, and white tights. Except for my uncle and his wife (the only representatives of my mom's family, since my grandmother had passed away two years before), all the guests were Black. Many of my dad's lieutenants and peers from the numbers business were in attendance, including Mr. Tom, my father's pony-tailed, foul-mouthed running buddy; Mr. Horace; and Mr. Reds.

I don't know when my parents' work together in the numbers business crossed the line into the personal. My mother was always less than forthcoming about the timeline (and I certainly lacked the courage to ask my father). When I was in fifth grade and looking through their wedding album, I broached the subject with my mother. "Why am I in these wedding photos?" I inquired.

"We had a private ceremony before you were born but decided to have a larger church ceremony later," my mother replied with a level gaze. My internal lie detector went off. It was clear she was not prepared to explain to a ten-year-old all the ways their relationship violated societal norms, so I let it drop.

As an adult, however, I understand from personal experience how relationships spring up unbidden and often defy courtesy and convenience. When my mother and father first met, he was separated from his wife Cora, the mother of most of his children; he was also caring for Megan's mother Judy, who was in home hospice and dying of a brain tumor. My dad's divorce from Cora wasn't official until I was three years old. No doubt his incarceration in 1977, the year I was born, had delayed its finalization, so 1981 was the earliest opportunity for my parents to marry.

On the surface, the differences between my mother's two marriages appear irreconcilable—a sharp, nonsensical zigzag in direction—but a bit of decoding exposes the underlying logic. As the child of working-class immigrants, my mother's sense of belonging was always tenuous; this made her identification with society's marginalized groups, including Black people, understandable. She told me how the other kids threw rocks at her own mother and called her "dirty Jew" back in the Transylvanian village where my grandma Sylvia was born. My mother's outsider status was also cemented by her name—the very ethnic-sounding Lussia (although her younger brother was given the Anglicized name Charles Newton). Plus there was the fact that my mother didn't think of herself as "white" in the strictest sense of the word. She described herself by her religion and ethnicity: "I was born Jewish, and I'll die Jewish," she told the Jehovah's Witnesses and Mormon missionaries who came to the house to proselytize.

Mom graduated from Calvin Coolidge High School in 1956, a mere two years after the *Brown v. Board of Education* decision. (Incidentally, this was the same year Marvin Gaye dropped out of one of DC's three "colored" high schools to join the army.) Her high school yearbook reveals a starkly homogeneous environment; the students' surnames are mostly Jewish, Italian, and Greek—the nonwhite whites of the city. There are no Black or brown teachers. The school's only Black employee pictured is Rosa Lee Bradley, who received accolades for the "good cakes and pies we eat at Coolidge" but stares at the camera with dead eyes. Among the hundreds of faces in my mom's senior class, I can find only one girl who is clearly African American (although some of the other students have darkish complexions). She wrote in my mom's yearbook: "Best of luck to a girl with beautiful hair." I see this Black classmate as a harbinger of my existence. Did this friendship embolden my mother to cross the color line? "Did you ever think you'd be flipping through Black hair magazines with your daughter?" I teased my mother during a visit to Barnes & Noble more than forty years later. Her smile was enigmatic.

My mother likely understood in some small way the loneliness of that Black student. She herself didn't have many friends because she couldn't identify with the Jewish kids who came from two-parent families with more disposable income and nicer things. "I found them to be snobbish and cliquish," she told me with hurt

140 *The Guardian*

in her eyes. Her best friends were a Jewish girl named Esther, who lived down the street in a humble apartment building with her grandmother, and Vivian Pappas, a hirsute Greek girl. By the time she was fourteen, my mother had stepped into the role of a quasi-adult, cooking dinner for her younger brother and making sure he did his homework. She even taught herself how to drive.

It was at Coolidge that my mother met Alvin. His family had escaped the Nazi invasion of Poland and fled to the Amalfi Coast during World War II. Alvin emerged from the ordeal unscathed, but as an adult, he couldn't resist the pull of the underworld. Unlike his younger American-born brother, who became a law-abiding accountant, Alvin gravitated to a career in sports betting and related underworld activities. On the frequent occasions he became embroiled in the criminal justice system, he was fond of playing the Holocaust survivor card to garner leniency. And perhaps because of his family's stint in Italy, he fancied himself gangster-adjacent and was fascinated by Mafia figures, especially Al Capone. One of the detectives who arrested him in 2002 for sports betting offered a more realistic rendering of Alvin's behavior: "There wasn't any leg-breaking. We have not seen any evidence of any violence [just] a lot of intimidation, yelling and screaming. Alvin gives off like he's a tough guy, but I'd be hard-pressed to say he's Mafia."[3] Alvin introduced my mother to the world of gambling. She and Alvin owned laundromats that they used to "clean" their money—just like Alvin's mafioso hero, who is credited with originating the term *money laundering.*

Between Alvin and my father there was Bill, my mother's first Black boyfriend. This might have been around the time she was stopped in a car with her Black friends and called a nigger by a white DC policeman, because why else would she be in a car with Black people? Maybe Bill was riding in the front seat with her. Bill's name occasionally came up when my parents argued. My dad's face would contort with jealousy as he screamed, "Why didn't you stay with that ugly motherfucker Bill? That bum!"

But according to my mother, Bill was just a harmless guy from rural North Carolina. The 5th Dimension's cover of "Wedding Bell

Blues," with Marilyn McCoo sweetly singing "Would you marry me Bill?" inevitably popped into my head whenever she mentioned him. I filed Bill away for reference, and some years later he came up unexpectedly when I had lunch with Alvin during my law firm years. "It was Bill, not your dad, that broke your grandmother's heart," he told me as he sighed and folded his small manicured hands. Grandma Sylvia hadn't been pleased about my mother's relationship with a Gentile, especially a Black man. Until my grandmother's death in 1979, my mom would take me to visit Grandma Sylvia, who fed me hard-boiled eggs. My father never accompanied us. When Alvin revealed that Bill had died during a drug-related dispute, I wondered which was the worse sin in my grandmother's eyes: being with a Black man or being with a drug dealer. She apparently kept silent about Alvin's criminal enterprise.

My mother first spied my father while driving down 14th Street and Florida Avenue, where he conducted the majority of his business. I flushed with embarrassment whenever she replayed the scene of her rolling down the driver's side window and exclaiming, "Oh man, that is a nice-looking guy." But at least in front of us children, my parents' relationship was not a physically affectionate one.

What particular charms did my father hold for my mother? If I'm being honest, this remains a bit of a mystery to me. My father was handsome and suave—when he wanted to turn it on and was in control of his temper. I could see that my mother responded differently to his jests: her face flushed, and her laughter came from lower down in her belly. He was also a great giver of gifts—flowers, clothing, jewelry. But I didn't see any real signs of intimacy, at least the way it was portrayed in the movies, with kissing, embracing, and tender whisperings.

I was in the fifth grade when I first glimpsed evidence of their intimacy. I was looking for a box of childhood keepsakes stored on the upper shelf of my parents' closet. Amidst my mother's packets of hosiery, purses, and bags of photographs, I uncovered a small book I had never seen before. In it, my dad had overlaid love poems on pastel pictures of beachscapes. Included with the poetry were lyrics from Bill Withers's "Ain't No Sunshine." I quickly slapped the cover closed, as if the pages had seared my hand. I was suddenly worried what would happen if he found out I had violated their privacy. This book filled with my dad's private musings revealed a different man from the one whose unpredictable outbursts frightened us. Was this the same person who called my mother a bitch, slammed her against the wall, and throttled her when he was having a bad day?

Despite this despicable treatment, my mother rarely felt sorry for herself. She told me quite candidly that, compared to her forebears, she was fortunate. She'd point to her grandmother, Bella Orleans. Bella's husband, David, left her behind while he traveled to America to pave the way for his family. "How the hell did my grandmother travel through Europe alone with six kids?" she'd ask as she shook her head in wonder.

If I had to guess, I think she extended this notion to my father, a Black child of the Jim Crow and Depression era who fought for a segregated navy and came back from the war to find that nothing had changed for him—or for Black Americans in general. Like the devoted Desdemona enamored of the older, battle-hardened general Othello, my mother "gave [my father] for [his] pains a world of sighs / She loved [him] for the dangers [he] had passed"—for the experiences that were the core of his identity.[4]

Unfortunately, my father didn't always view my mother's empathetic nature as a virtue. "White people, they'll cry over a dog, but they'll lynch a nigger," was one of his frequent refrains. Despite the historical truth of his comment, I could not for the life of me comprehend how he equated my Jewish mother with a lynch mob. I'd shake my head in disbelief and mutter, "If she is such a villain, why stay with her?"

Notwithstanding her exceedingly high tolerance threshold and empathy for my father, even my mother had her limits. She was human, after all. As an eight-year-old, I watched through the kitchen doorway as she lobbed china down the basement stairs after one of their arguments, stunned by the sound of breaking plates. I was accustomed to my father entering the house on a rampage, shaking the foundations like a whipping wind as he seized objects (or people) to smash against the walls (including grapefruit halves that left a permanent stain on the flowered wallpaper in the living room). But this memory of my mother made such a stark impression precisely because it was not the usual way she reacted to his violence.

My father was a complex figure. Like Othello, he was a Black man of dignity and intelligence who had been "objectifie[d] . . . so relentlessly" by white society that he became "un-incorporable in that world."[5] This caused him to opt out of a white economy that degraded him. But like the Moor, he tragically lost his reason. His response to the violence surrounding him—the extreme violence of child abuse, racism, poverty, and war—transformed him into an unhinged perpetrator who directed his anger toward the person dearest to him.[6] At these times, his self-loathing (an inner Iago) urged him to see my mother through a distorted lens of mistrust and enmity.

The Protector

When I was a newly walking, wobbly legged toddler on Evarts Street, I was defenseless against the teenagers who rode their bikes recklessly on the sidewalk in front of our house, threatening to mow me down. After issuing a few admonishments that were ignored, my mother stretched out her arm and knocked one of them off the bike as they came racing down the block. Over the years, whenever she told this story, it always brought a conspicuous and mischievous glint to her eyes.

After the more pedestrian dangers of my toddler years, the biggest threat came from within myself. Between the ages of four and eight, I suffered from severe asthma attacks. Upon hearing the telltale wheeze as my airway constricted, my mother would snatch me up, throw me in the car, and race me to nearby Children's Hospital. These attacks were often triggered by something as mundane as a cold drink or an Italian ice. (I remember one time we returned from the hospital and my cherry-flavored ice had melted and left a bright pink stain on the living room carpet, which my mother could never scrub out.) I would have to remain at the hospital for several hours (but never overnight), until my breathing normalized. The nurses were kind and gave me room-temperature ginger ale to drink. My mother would sit next to my bed in the room filled with other asthmatic children like me, concern wrinkling her brow.

I learned that two wildly different things can be true at once. On the one hand, my mother was my forceful protector, my ever-vigilant guardian; on the other hand, she was my father's pitiable victim. When it came to defending us kids, she was sharp-tongued and unafraid, acting as both a literal and a figurative shield between us and our father. But when it came to protecting herself, it was a different story. It was impossible for me to reconcile these two sides of my mother.

Unlike some of my schoolmates' parents at Sidwell, my mother did not believe in the Socratic method of parenting. "These new-school parents do too much talking and explaining," she'd gripe when we encountered a parent in a grocery store trying to gently coax a recalcitrant child into behaving. "Everything doesn't have to be a discussion. Just tell that kid to cut it out!" In the relatively rare instances when I was impertinent or pesky, she'd smack the top of my head with a plastic-handled hairbrush or restrain me by the back of the neck. One day when I wouldn't stop whining about my broken Barbie doll, she tossed it out the car window (a move she later felt guilty about). Eventually I could tell when I had crossed a line by the pitch of her voice or her vicious side eye.

I spent a lot of time with my mother, especially as my older siblings started to move out of the house. Our favorite haunts were the old Hot Shoppes cafeterias, with their glutinous chicken soup and red Jell-O cups with whipped cream spirals; Roy Rogers, where I nibbled on the crispy skin of the fried chicken breasts while my mom doused her roast beef sandwiches in barbecue sauce; and the Little Tavern, with its green swivel bar stools and miniature hamburgers on slightly sweet potato rolls. Although she cared for all of us, in certain ways my mother set me apart from the other children in the family. She gave me a host of nicknames—some logical (Nisha), and others more inventive (Zeedee, or Z for short). She carefully coordinated my hair ribbons with my dresses. And she sniffed my neck to wake me up and then put socks on me so I wouldn't have to step on the cold hardwood floor barefoot.

Because I was her only biological child, she transmitted her Jewish culture to me—largely through my diet. I was the only kid who accompanied her to the Chesapeake Bagel Bakery on Sunday

146   *The Guardian*

mornings. I watched with fascination as the freshly baked bagels rolled off the conveyor belt, destined for toasting and a schmear of cream cheese. She brought me paper packages of smoked whitefish, their brassy, iridescent scales glistening; then she would surgically remove the bones so that I could safely consume the moist morsels of flesh. I ate chopped liver with gusto and consumed spoonfuls of sour cream, with or without mouthfuls of blintzes or latkes.

People often remarked on our verbal resemblance, even more so than our physical resemblance. My mother had a distinctive molasses cadence that was a blend of DC accent (*Warshington* instead of *Washington* and *ratiator* instead of *raydiator*) with Eastern European inflections (*singer*, with emphasis on the *g*) and Yiddish words I could pronounce but couldn't spell (for instance, her word for the ultimate *balabusta* [good homemaker], which sounded like *TY-ree*). She also had some old-school vocabulary that definitely stood out among my peers' parents (pocketbook for purse, dungarees for jeans). College friends from the Northeast thought she sounded Southern, but my Black friends from the mid-Atlantic who were unfamiliar with ethnically Jewish accents thought she had a slight New York accent. Although my voice was (and still is) higher pitched, I absorbed identical inflections. I also unwittingly developed her habit of swearing. I didn't realize that other children my age weren't supposed to use such words until I heard my best friend's strict Trinidadian father suck his teeth at one of the *fucks* I let fly so freely. I asked my mother about using cuss words, and she told me, "If it's the worst thing you do in life, you've got nothing to worry about." When it came to language, she was laissez-faire, as long as it wasn't ill-intentioned.

What she could not abide was bullying. It was one thing for my father to come after her, but she would not stand by and watch one of "hers" be harmed. Although my father's lawyer credited him as being "responsible for the emotional stability of [his] children at a time when the family group has endured an extraordinary degree of pressure and severe loss," my mother often assumed this role for both her child and her stepchildren. The motion asking for a reduction of my dad's sentence specifically referenced the therapy my brother Johnny received for panic attacks. It was my mother who arranged for counseling and shuttled Johnny to his appointments at a time when therapy for children was not widely embraced. It was my mother who intervened (to her detriment) when my father got too rough with his adolescent sons, mistaking them for grown men who could defend themselves. And it was my mother who took the beating when some payoff money went missing, even though it was my brother who stole it from her purse.

In my early years, it was my mother who egged me on when I confronted an elementary school bully. My best friend Adrienne was a timid, chubby girl with the rounded pink cheeks of a cartoon character. We met at St. Ann's when we were four years old. This was my first telephonic friendship—I still remember how excited I was when, with my mother's guidance, I carefully punched out Adrienne's number on the square buttons of the basement phone. In first grade, our classroom bully Helen began stealing my friend's crayons and other school supplies, provoking tears and generally making life miserable for this sensitive soul. To make matters worse, the teacher seemed oblivious to Helen's shenanigans.

I decided to take matters into my own hands and formed an alliance with my classmate Timothy, a petite, light-skinned boy with an unusually deep voice and peach fuzz on his upper lip. One of Helen's go-to moves was to pull the chair out from under people, so we decided to give her a taste of her own medicine. Unfortunately, the teacher happened to be watching when Helen landed with the desired thud on the carpeted floor and tried to laugh off her fall from grace. Timothy and I were immediately upbraided and sent home with the assignment to write an apology letter to Helen, to be delivered the next day.

I came home troubled and shared what had happened with my mom. I was beginning to feel slightly remorseful, based on the teacher's harsh reaction. To my surprise, my mother looked at me and said in her deep voice, "You are *not* writing a letter to *that* girl." So I didn't. The next day, I arrived at school feeling secure in my decision, and when the teacher instructed me to hand over my letter, I replied with determination, "My mom told me not to write that letter." The funny thing is, Timothy's parents gave him the same advice. The teacher, not appreciating these acts of insubordination, canceled recess for the two of us and forced us to write the letters anyway.

I went home with my tail between my legs and told my mom about the teacher's reaction. I don't recall her exact response, but I bet it included some choice cuss words. The next day she and my father arrived at the school, their tightly compressed mouths indicating their displeasure. Nobody in their right mind wanted to face the wrath of an incensed Lussia and John Matthews if they knew what was good for them. I don't know what transpired during that teacher-parent conference, but the teacher came out looking wilted and grim. And that was the end of the "Helen troubles."

Likewise, my mother went over my eighth-grade mathematics teacher's head when the teacher recommended (for the first time) that I not be placed in the tier one math track. Her reasoning was not that I couldn't do the work or that my grades weren't good enough but that I had taken too many sick days and wouldn't be able to "keep up" in high school. My mother learned from talking to some of the other parents that the teacher had declined to recommend other students of color to Math I as well. So she made an appointment with the middle school principal to discuss the matter. "Johnisha has been in the top class all four years," she said. "And now, all of a sudden, this woman is trying to say she can't keep up? I don't think so!" The principal must have agreed, because the following year those other students and I were permitted to take Math I.

My mother didn't hesitate to call out other parents either. Although I typically didn't attend sleepovers, she had reluctantly agreed to let me spend the night at my sixth-grade classmate's house, and it was the first and last time I visited that family's home. When my mother came to pick me up late the next morning, the other mother pointedly asked her: "Does Johnisha stay up late all the time? I was trying to get the girls to settle down and she was whispering late into the night." Instead of perceiving me as a harmless and overexcited eleven-year-old, the mother implied that I was hyperactive and troublesome.

"No. No she doesn't. She just doesn't get to sleep over a lot," my mom responded with a pronounced bite.

As we walked to the car, my mother erupted: "What does she think we do, just stay up and play music all night and party? How does she think you get better grades than her daughter?" she scoffed. "These white people have some nerve!"

When I was still in high school, my older siblings were now adults, living on their own and focused on bills, partners, and children. I saw them on holidays and occasional visits, but I didn't enjoy close relationships with anyone except Megan, who attended college in Chicago.

Growing up, Megan and I had many dustups because we were vastly different temperamentally and seven years apart in age. I was the fly she wanted to swat or, in more bruising moments, the cockroach she wanted to grind with the heel of her shoe. But then shortly before she left for college, our relationship began to change. Around this same time she adopted the name Mejudi, a combination of her name and that of her late mother, Judy. She also took me into her confidence about her unrequited crushes and tried to explain what it meant to be a "mod" (as far as I could tell, it entailed wearing solid black and writing mopey poetry). We sat in her bedroom and listened to the melancholy music spinning on her turntable—the Cure, the Smiths, the Velvet Underground, and Kate Bush. After she left for college, we had marathon phone calls, and she made recordings for me with handwritten liner notes folded into the clear plastic cases—what she called "Nisha mixes."

With Megan gone, my mother and I were alone in the house with my father, with only ourselves to rely on. I started talking back to him—what he called sassing. It was a risky strategy, but it was effective as long as I was still "girlish" enough for my dad to restrain himself from pummeling me. However, having witnessed the beatings my siblings had received, I knew this period of inviolability wouldn't last forever; the more I started to resemble a grown woman, the more threatening I would become to him. "I'm going to take you down a buttonhole or two lower," he would glower. These words may have sounded quaint in someone else's mouth, but not in my father's. I was the one line in the sand for my mother. "If you touch her," she yelled when he threatened me, "that is the end of you."

My other tactic to protect my mother was to become the most trouble-free child possible. I knew that all of Megan's rebellious teenage acts—such as arguing vociferously with our parents, drinking, and breaking into her friend's mother's house when she was on vacation—redounded on my mother. In effect, she became the scapegoat—a human version of the animal in Jewish atonement rituals that assumes the sins of an entire community. As a result, I readily surrendered to the strict limits placed on me. I didn't have a curfew in high school because I never stayed out late. I didn't drink or go to parties or get in trouble with my friends because the person who would suffer most was not me but my mother. She would have to deal with my father's belligerence, his name-calling, his blame for my bad decisions, and, on the worst nights, his violence. My obedience, along with my scholastic achievement, was a paltry offering, but it was all I had to try to keep my mother safe.

I lived with the outsized guilt of not doing enough, and I developed a new and strangely unnerving symptom: Imagine being in bed, sleeping but not sleeping. You want to move, but your arms and legs are leaden and refuse to obey. Your breath is shallow as you attempt to scream, but your voice is barely a kittenish whimper. You are convinced that if you don't wake up, you will die. When you finally manage to wake yourself, you are too terrified to fall back to sleep. I didn't know what to call this phenomenon at the time, but what I was experiencing is called sleep paralysis. During REM sleep, the muscles relax as a protective mechanism so that you don't strike out and inadvertently hurt yourself during vivid dreams. With sleep paralysis, however, this so-called atonia persists in a state of wakefulness. During these episodes, chest-pressure hallucinations, also called incubus hallucinations, account for the sensation of suffocation that feels all too real. No one knows what causes sleep paralysis, but it is linked to anxiety disorders. After nights of sleep disrupted by this strange phenomenon, I frequently fell asleep during my midafternoon classes, when the fatigue overwhelmed me.

But sleep paralysis was only a prelude to what I experienced at Harvard. After losing my second oldest sister Renee to breast cancer in my sophomore year, I found that Cambridge's foreshortened winter days plunged me into a deep depression. I developed debilitating stomach pains, and during my junior year I sometimes felt so low that I didn't want to leave my dorm room. Out of concern, my boyfriend Dmitri called my mother. Despite the fragile state of my parents' household, she didn't hesitate to take the long train ride up to Massachusetts. She stayed with me, sleeping on a cot in my dorm room, until I started to improve. Her presence did not instantly alleviate my depression, but her love made me feel safe. Years later at my mother's funeral, my college roommate told me, "My mother would have never done that for me."

I knew I was fortunate to be loved so deeply by her. I had often told my mother, "If something happens to you, I would just prefer to die than have to face life without you." I honestly didn't think I could survive a permanent separation.

Bashert

If my mother hadn't intervened ever so gently, I might not be happily married. Or maybe my marriage was part of the good fortune foretold by that old Chinese lady.

With the marked exception of Dmitri, my dating history had a troubling pattern: I usually put forth more effort and became more emotionally invested than the other person. I replicated the male love I had witnessed in my own life—a male love that was distant, conditional, and erratic, a male love that demeaned and rejected you but pulled you back when it suited. In theory, I yearned for a different kind of partner—a loving partner who was consistent, nurturing, and protective but not controlling. For the most part, I had experienced this kind of love only from women, and when I found it in Dmitri, I recoiled out of distrust of the love itself and distrust of myself as a worthy recipient. But that type of male love did exist, and it found me only after I had done the necessary work to defeat the inner voice that ensnared me in my eating disorder.

In early October 2005, my mother waited on a young man named Andy at the fragrance counter of the department store where she worked. While chatting about his plans for graduate school, they discovered that they both had close relatives who were attorneys and that they actually worked at the same law firm (but in different departments). It was one of those DC-is-a-small-town moments. The customer left with the cologne samples my mother gave out with abandon to people she liked, and the two of them shared the story of the serendipitous meeting with their attorney relatives.

Almost a month later, my coworker and friend Saminaz invited me to attend the corporate department's happy hour. I had initially declined the invitation because I had other plans, and besides, as a litigation associate, I didn't know many people in the corporate department. I ended up going only because my friend canceled our dinner plans at the last minute. At happy hour I met Jon, Andy's handsome, dark-haired, aquamarine-eyed brother, and we spent half an hour chatting. The story of our relatives meeting by chance was a good conversation starter, but we found an easy cadence. I liked that he didn't take himself as seriously as most of the other younger male attorneys at the firm.

This was the second time I had the sensation that I had met someone who would be important in my life. From the start, I felt a strange cosmic spark between Jon and me. I believe that sometimes the universe "knows" something before your rational mind is aware of it. But I already had a boyfriend, and we were currently on round two. After breaking up with me, he had asked for a second chance. My initial instinct had been to move on, but his persistence convinced me that maybe things would be different this time around. Nevertheless, I thought enough of my first encounter with Jon to show my mom his picture on the law firm's website. She gave me a nod of approval, and I laughed. Unbeknownst to me at the time, when Jon went home to New Hampshire to attend a family friend's wedding, he told his father, "I met a woman."

Jon and I developed a friendship over the next few months, as I found my relationship with my boyfriend less and less emotionally fulfilling. He wasn't intentionally selfish, but we were wholly mismatched when it came to emotional intelligence and maturity. When I contrasted my friendship with Jon, who was a few years older and knew what he wanted and wasn't afraid to go after it, my current relationship's shortcomings became more obvious. I treasured Jon's thoughtfulness and kindheartedness, his empathetic nature. In many ways he reminded me of my mother and how she wholeheartedly loved the people in her life. Although we were raised quite differently, our values were compatible, and we shared a cultural identity. Although neither of us was observantly Jewish and both of us had dated outside of our race and religion, certain intangible qualities make some people feel a little more like home than others. Jon and I had that in each other. It was the first time I had found this quality in a man.

Within two months, things came to a head. I needed some distance from my friendship with Jon to decide what was right for me. Did I stay with my boyfriend, or did I leave him? If I left, would Jon and I give our relationship a try? When I hesitatingly told Jon I needed time apart from him, he told me, "Don't worry. I'm not going anywhere. When you are ready to talk again, I will be here for you. I understand what you are doing, and I respect you."

One weekend during this self-imposed separation, my mother and I wandered the cobbled streets of Old Town Alexandria and passed by the Bittersweet Café, with its inviting green awning. We immediately zoomed in on the dessert display of pastel confections and wordlessly agreed that it was lunchtime. As we consumed our sandwiches and then peeled back the cupcake wrappers and mashed our faces into the tender crumb and mile-high frosting, I attempted to work through my angst. I listened to what my mother said and what she didn't say. If anyone knew me, it was her. If anyone wanted me to be happy, it was her. She had already met Jon on a number of occasions. The first time, he had gone into the department store where she worked and stopped by to introduce himself. As he approached the counter, she pronounced, "I know you. You are Jon Levi. I recognize you from the photograph Johnisha showed me." When I found out, I tried not to worry too much about Jon thinking I was some kind of stalker. "He was so patient," Mom told me. "I had some customers around, and he just said, 'No rush, take your time.'" It was admittedly a small thing, but when you are married to a man who waits for nothing, a man who kicks your car door for being a few minutes late, you pay attention to those subtle indicators of a person's character.

And so my mother heard me out at lunch. "I'm used to being the one hurt in a relationship, and if I break it off with my boyfriend, I would be the one inflicting harm," I explained with great anguish.

She drew in a deep breath and said gently, "I don't want to see you make a mistake because you are too concerned about hurting another person. I think you have the chance to be truly happy. Some people just make you feel like you are walking on air, and you deserve a chance at something like that."

I went home and weighed her words over the next few days. She had been direct without being pushy. I ultimately decided that I had to do the painful thing because there was likely something better waiting for me past the discomfort and the guilt. Once I had ended the relationship with my boyfriend, I was free to explore the future with Jon. Within a few weeks after our first real date, Jon told me that he loved me. I was astonished and responded in kind, but the idea of love being so easy was foreign to me. I wasn't used to having a man reveal his heart to me and show unabashed affection for me. I saw it in the smallest of gestures, such as his daily emails that always ended with "I love you" (and still do to this day), and his tenderness when anything small (a carping partner) or large (my ongoing struggle to beat back thoughts of my unworthiness) aggrieved me. I saw it in the way he pulled his chair closer to mine when we were among family and friends. Even more so than with my mother, I could share all my fears and worries with Jon, without being judged or rebuffed and without feeling alone and misunder-stood, let alone ridiculed.

Although my mother championed Jon, I was anxious about my father's reaction to the new man in my life. They shared nearly the same name and had the same birthday, exactly fifty years apart. It was a strange omen, given how dissimilar they were in so many other ways. Yet my new boyfriend, like my father, was a clothes-horse; more substantially, they shared an old-fashioned sense of what it means to give your word to others.

Their first meeting wasn't as disastrous as I expected, but my dad wasn't particularly warm either. My parents sat in the car outside the

156   *The Guardian*

law firm one day, intending to meet me after work. Jon and I came out, and my mother greeted him, turned to my father, and said, "John, are you going to say hi to Jon, Johnisha's new boyfriend?"

My dad, presiding in the front seat as if it were a lofty throne, deigned to cast a side glance at Jon before pronouncing huffily, "I'm eighty-two years old! If he wants to speak, he can say hello."

I waited for the scene to turn ugly, but Jon handled my dad's sarcasm with aplomb, even as my mom began to protest. "No, Lussia, he's correct," Jon said as he approached the window on the passenger side. "Hi Mr. Matthews. I'm Jon Levi, it's very nice to meet you."

"How do you do," my dad replied, seemingly satisfied that he had been validated.

And it was at that moment that I knew Jon could handle both me and my family.

In 2008, two years after Jon and I met, my mother would speak at our wedding in the small town of Ludlow, Vermont. When Jon asked my parents' permission to marry me, my father seemed a bit distracted at first, so my mother nudged him for a reaction. "It's about time you asked," he responded. "Now I don't have to support Johnisha anymore." It's unclear whether he was just being a wise guy or if that was the time warp of his dementia speaking, since I was thirty years old and hadn't been financially supported by my parents for quite a while.

Despite stormy bookends, the day turned out mild and sunny for the duration of the wedding festivities—perfect for an outdoor ceremony. My father was in a playful mood once he recovered from some dizziness and nausea the night before. He let me photograph him wearing Jon's black velvet yarmulke, and he spent most of the reception gracefully whisking women across the dance floor to jazz standards. Everyone wanted a turn to dance with him! (The other guests were unaware that, at the end of the night, he turned to me and declared in complete and utter seriousness, "Somebody should have a party here. This would be a nice place for it.")

Before the ceremony, we gathered to sign the *ketubah*, the Jewish marriage contract. Instead of the arcane language that appeared in my grandmother's and mother's contracts, we substituted a highly personal "Letter to My *Bashert*," the Hebrew word for soulmate:

> In a single day, my life changed. That day was November 5, 2005. From the beginning, you and I were like old friends. So comfortable, so familiar. It could only be that you were the one.
>
> Now with you, my best friend by my side, every joy is magnified, every fear ephemeral, and every misfortune transcended.
>
> Each new day is an occasion to celebrate how you made my life, a canvas on which to share our dreams, and an opportunity to affirm our deep commitment to each other.
>
> In this marriage, each finds voice in the other. Equal, even, at home, on base, you are always my favorite place. Cheek to cheek, we will face life in welcome embrace. You breathe, I listen. We will love well and life will glisten. These are the promises that we make to each other today.

My mother was elegant in a silver knit top and matching silk skirt that highlighted her short salt-and-pepper hair as she stood to give her speech at the evening reception. She described the day's event as "the most joyous occasion" of her life and then shared a brief story about the day I was born, quickly skipping ahead to my adult years. "Being the Jewish mother that I am, there was a weight on me that said, 'What if something happens to me and Johnisha doesn't have anyone to care for her?' Then, answering my prayers, came Jon!" She claimed to know pretty quickly that Jon was meant to be her son-in-law. "And so," she concluded with gusto, "a heavy weight came off me because after I knew him, I knew that he was going to take care of Johnisha, and that she was going to take care of him. And now she's in good hands and I don't have to worry anymore!"

Whenever I replay my wedding video, I glimpse both my mother's past and her future. The past is how she almost lost me, how I might have slipped so easily from her grasp when she was arrested for violating her probation in 1977. And the future is that, in seven years' time, after surviving so much, she would be taken from me by a cancer that was already taking root.

The Diagnosis

My mother believed the cancer planted itself in her body at the time of Megan's death and drew its nourishment from her stress and grief. Like other large families, ours experienced a seemingly disproportionate amount of personal tragedy—my sister Renee's death from breast cancer in her forties, Megan's death, my father's disappearance, and Michael's fatal aortic rupture. I sometimes thought of the Matthews family as the Black Kennedys (minus the fortune and the trust funds).

When I was a third-year law associate, the year before I married, Megan lost consciousness at her home in Evanston, Illinois, and was rushed to the hospital. She had a misdiagnosed pulmonary embolism; she had been told the pain in her upper chest and arm was due to pneumonia and had been sent home without any scans. I was out in Spokane participating in an arbitration when I got the news, so I left the team and rushed to Chicago. My mother, my sister Marilyn, and my father's cousin kept a days-long vigil over Megan's hospital bed. Eventually, the doctors informed us that she no longer displayed any brain activity, and my mother and I made the heart-wrenching decision to withdraw life support. Megan was only thirty-six years old.

Although we all mourned Megan, my mother was utterly consumed by grief for the little girl she had helped raise. For the first time in my life, my mother felt very far away from me. All her conversations began and ended with her crushing guilt about a life cut short. She lamented my sister's fragile existence as a divorced mother fending off an ex-husband who verbally harassed and threatened her. "He pushed her and pushed her," she told anyone who would listen. "It was too much strain on her system. Maybe she would have taken better care of herself if not for him. Maybe she would have gotten better medical care. I blame him and his family. They always enabled him." My father's dementia was so advanced that he couldn't fully grasp Megan's death. He sometimes asked how she was doing or called me by her name. As a consequence, my mother could find no solace in their mutual sorrow.

Who is to say that my mother was wrong about the origins of her cancer? The power of grief can unmake a person in different ways, and maybe that includes co-opting a person's cells. It was ovarian cancer, so the source of my life became the source of my mother's gradual and inevitable demise.

Her first indication that something wasn't right was the sensation of her intestines "freezing." She had always been good at reading the body's clues and signposts—her own as well as mine—so she knew her symptoms went beyond simple constipation.

The first doctor she consulted advised her to add more fiber to her diet. She disregarded this advice and sought a second opinion because, having lived in her body for more than seventy years, she knew the solution was not Metamucil. The second doctor performed more tests and scans, confirming my mother's intuition. It wasn't what she wanted to hear. The cancer was stage 3, and the tumor in her ovary was so large that it had affected the function of her intestines. The tumor cells had also migrated to her bladder.

I learned the seriousness of my mother's condition while living in Charlotte and attending culinary school. I had been laid off by the law firm during the recession, and once the shock and anger wore off, I realized that this professional crisis presented an opportunity to reset my life. With Jon's encouragement, and after much soul-searching, research, and some hands-on experience, I decided to pursue a longtime passion of mine for the culinary arts. Jon and I lived apart for the ten months it took to complete my degree at Johnson & Wales University. When my mother broke the news that she needed surgery to remove a malignant ovarian tumor as well as her uterus, she was confident about her chances. She was prepared to undergo the most aggressive measures to give herself the best shot at recovery. "I think I'm going to be okay," she explained calmly and convincingly. "I trust my oncologist and the surgeon, and after the surgery, we will follow up with chemotherapy to ensure that we haven't missed anything and that it doesn't come back."

My guilt over being away from home at such a critical time was crushing. To assuage me, Jon and I worked out a schedule. He would visit my mother daily during her hospital recovery and keep close tabs on her thereafter. I would return home on the weekends as often as I could, but if I missed too many classes, I would have to repeat those units. The weekend of the surgery, I explained to the stern but kindly German chef who taught my chocolate class that I needed to miss a day of instruction to be by my mother's side.

My mom came out of surgery weak but resolved. She lost a lot of blood and required multiple transfusions, and the tumor was larger than anticipated. It took her a while to regain her strength. She took about six weeks off work but returned to the department store while undergoing her chemotherapy treatments.

When I graduated from culinary school in May 2011, my mother and father made the trip to Charlotte so we could all celebrate the day together. Mom never missed one of my graduations or other major milestones. Although her close-cropped, thinning hair was a telltale sign of cancer, I hadn't seen her so joyful and relaxed in a long time. My mother-in-law and father-in-law also flew to Charlotte for the celebration. This graduation was a cathartic do-over for me, given my disastrous law school graduation. Conversation flowed between the two sets of parents, and my father was full of good humor at dinner. He even tried Indian food and enjoyed it—a first! I took a photo of my parents and realized how much they had come to resemble each other, with their oblong faces, fine features, and sparse hair. Later that night Jon and I took everyone to the Ritz-Carlton to hear my favorite local vocalist, and my dad displayed a few of his dance moves.

Following my graduation, Jon and I had to make a decision about relocation. The job prospects for him were dim in Charlotte, so he had applied for a position at a small Boston law firm. He was ready to step away from "big law" in the next phase of his career, and a culinary career was readily transferable, so I didn't mind. I was optimistic about my mom's condition, given her good spirits and the positive prognosis from her oncologist.

Tragedy brought us home again when my father disappeared and was subsequently found in Rock Creek Park. The day of his memorial service was in many ways a testament to my mother's strength. I found myself watching her with a sense of awe at her will to survive. She greeted people with warmth and circulated in the Black Catholic church with ease. She gripped my hand when I was nervous about speaking at the service and offered to accompany me. She was delighted when she recognized friends of my older siblings who had come to pay their respects. She made sure people knew that there was food in the building across the way and that they would be well fed. My old law firm colleagues and friends remarked on how strong and composed she was. The words "incredible," "lady," "grace," and "strong," were like bubbles floating above her head.

My mom was at her best when she was caring for other people, and she spent most of the day comforting those who had come to say good-bye to my father. She drew strength from the people who had congregated that day, whereas I felt ground down by the flood of emotion pouring out of them. But I knew, from our private moments, that my father's passing devastated my mother. With my brother by her side, she went to the park where his body had been discovered to say her private and anguished good-bye.

As much as I struggled to understand how and why my parents' relationship endured, my mom believed in their love story. It wasn't the love story I would have chosen for her, but I had to accept that it wasn't my choice. She refused to leave him in life, and she would not part with his ashes either, taking them to Boston after she sold the family house. Whether I liked it or not, my dad had been her life. Now, all she had left was me.

The Diagnosis 163

I had convinced my mom to sell her house, which required more and more upkeep. The same house that had felt too small and bursting at the seams when two parents and at least four children lived in it now felt cavernous and empty to her. It was filled with the mementos of a former life, many of which were too painful to hold on to. She hired professionals to clean it out. The 1970s-era brown-and-white World Book encyclopedias and my parents' extensive record and eight-track collections from the basement would have to go, as well as the miscellaneous books (including Shakespeare) in the attic and the twenty or more Cabbage Patch dolls packed away in boxes. However, when she relocated to Boston, my mom brought along many of the papers I had written in middle and high school, including my seventh-grade report on Dred Scott, as well as all the memorabilia from my youth orchestra's trips to Jordan. She kept a few of my Pauline and Madame Alexander dolls and my first doll, Beebee (my pronunciation of "baby"), whose neck was broken and whose blond hair had been hacked too short in my attempts to play hairdresser. She also brought along the family portrait of her grandparents and her mother, aunts, and uncles; a painting of her grandfather, David Orleans; and the large, eerily lifelike charcoal drawings of Megan and me by a New York City street artist when I was eight years old and she was fifteen. And although Mom parted with a lot of my father's clothing, she kept some sweaters that I discovered later when I cleaned out her condo. She never mentioned them, so having them must have been a secret comfort to her.

This was not only the house where my mother had raised her family; it was also the house where she had grown up. So she had to say good-bye to a string of ghosts accumulated through the decades of her life: her mother, her father, her little brother, my sister, and my father, all of whom had called this house their home.

It was up to me to find my mom a condo in Boston, and the real estate market was unrelentingly competitive. She wanted no part of living with Jon and me. "You need to have space as a couple," she argued repeatedly. I knew she was also reclaiming her independence. Now that my father was gone, she was no longer tethered

164   *The Guardian*

to his violence or his illness, even as she confronted her own mortality. She visited Boston just once to express her preferences before I selected a clean, affordable unit in a building a few miles from our house with accessible shopping and other conveniences that would allow her to live comfortably without pinching every penny. Sometimes she gave me crap about the incompetence of building maintenance or the tired-looking hall carpets, but all in all, she was satisfied with the new, smaller accommodations for her and her dog.

My mom's life in Boston was no doubt extended by a few years due to her participation in clinical trials at the Dana-Farber Cancer Institute, one of the premier cancer treatment and research facilities in the world. She spent a lot of time there and enjoyed the caregivers and the volunteers who stopped by to give hand rubs or have a chat or wheeled the book cart around for patients to select reading material. All the same, she never quite adjusted to Boston. The people were too rude, the streets too dirty (this particularly aggrieved her), and the weather too gray. There was *way* too much snow (she had me take a photo of a ten-foot-tall pile of plow-removed snow so she could share it with a friend back home). She grudgingly got to know some of the neighbors and loved the (Jewish) mailman, but mostly she just lived in peace with her dog. We visited each other multiple times a week, but our conversations were not as fluid as they once were; they were punctuated by long silences, both of us staring into space. No doubt this was at least partly a product of the grief and sense of mortality we were experiencing. By this point, I was becoming inured to family tragedy, and I seized up emotionally to protect myself. With each loss, I built a thicker carapace. Life was just too hard otherwise.

Whenever she asked me about my plans to have children, I got slightly hostile. I was much crankier than I had ever been with my mother in these moments. It was like I was going through a delayed adolescence, a belated cleaving. I was almost 100 percent certain I didn't want any children, despite fantasizing about being a mother in my twenties. Now that I was married, I felt a new sense of security and freedom. The love I had craved as a child was now mine; I no longer had to fight for it or compete for it. It pained me to realize that because of my lack of interest in becoming a parent, my mom thought I was somehow defective. She simply could not imagine anyone wanting to remain childless if they had a comfortable life and a loving partner. She made several appeals to me, always some variation of the following:

"I just think you are making a mistake. Do you want to be alone when you are old? I mean, what if something happened to Jon before you?" she'd ask.

"Mom, the fear of being lonely is kind of a selfish reason to decide to have a kid. You have to want to raise a kid. And anyway, there's no guarantee that your kid won't grow up to hate your guts and want nothing to do with you."

My mom's face would crumple in response. "Wouldn't it be nice to have someone to take care of you if you get ill? Where would I be if I didn't have you and Jon?"

By this time, my voice would assume a higher pitch. "I understand, but it still doesn't seem like a good enough reason on its own to have a child. All the complications and things that can happen, it scares me. I just wouldn't be happy right now."

She would reply, "Nothing is ever perfect. You would figure out what you need to figure out. I think sometimes you think too much about things."

These conversations concluded the same way every time. I would protest and get irritated at being so misunderstood. I had been granted an immense amount of love in my marriage. Wasn't it greedy (or tempting fate) to ask for more? I reveled in my husband's attention, and I wasn't convinced that adding another person to the arrangement would benefit either of us when life was already so extraordinary. It was sort of like the story my mother used to tell me about my grandmother drawing the perfect flower and then ruining it by trying to add a pot to the drawing. Shouldn't we leave well enough alone? We had the flower, and that was enough. And yet, I still had a small nagging doubt—not large enough to spur me to action, but enough to nibble at my convictions.

Good-bye

I knew my mom wouldn't live forever, but when her time came, the cresting wave of her illness swept my legs out from under me quite viciously. It was as if time had been fast-forwarded and I couldn't push a button to stop it or slow it down. For a few months she had been complaining of pain in her abdomen, but she was still responding to some of the experimental treatments. In the few short weeks between Columbus Day and December 8, 2015, the day she passed away, my mother spun from hospital to rehab to hospital again and finally to hospice.

Some deaths become markers in your life—the before and the after. I have recovered from every death that touched me, except for my mom's. This one threatened to unmake me, and in some ways it did. My mother was my first Valentine. (As adults, we continued to exchange gifts on this holiday. Because she had been a florist, she loved to send me impeccable long-stemmed roses.) My grief visits me during small moments of joy, when I know I can no longer share the news with my mom; in dark moments, when I realize I can't draw on her knowledge of my history and our shared pain; and in my dreams, where she appears too infrequently.

On a Saturday morning during the brunch shift at the restaurant where I was working, Jon got a call from my distressed mother. The medicine she had been taking to unblock her intestines had caused uncontrolled diarrhea and vomiting. She had been doubling up on the dosage, with catastrophic results. Over the next few frantic

166

hours, Jon would check her into Beth Israel Deaconess Medical Center, clean up the mess she had left in his car, and take her dog to the vet for short-term boarding. After a few harrowing weeks in the hospital and then a rehab facility, where she didn't improve as expected, we brought her back to Dana-Farber.

That night, she underwent a full body scan, and the next day her oncologist, Dr. Konstantinopoulous (we called him Dr. K), summoned us for a family conference. When we arrived, I saw that my mother looked more comfortable. A second oncologist, a dark-haired woman, was also present. "We wanted to discuss with you what we learned from last night's scan," Dr. K began. "Unfortunately, I have to tell you that the cancer has now spread to other parts of Lussia's body, including her lungs." He looked straight at my mom as he said these words: "And I'm sorry, but we have exhausted our treatment options at this point. We are going to need to start to discuss palliative care, and what we can do to make you most comfortable for the time that you have left."

"How long do I have left?" my mom asked. Remarkably, there was no quaver in her voice.

"Likely a month. Or less," Dr. K responded gently.

I started to wail and went limp. How had this happened so suddenly? We knew she was sick, but how had we gone from rehab to death in a matter of twenty-four hours? I started to think about all the things I would have done differently in the preceding weeks, had I known—all the words I would take back, all the additional time I would have spent, all the complaining I wouldn't have done.

As always, my mother was quick to leap to my defense. "I'm just worried about my child. You see how emotional she is." I will never forget what she said next, because it was so far removed from her own pain. "Dr. K, this must be very hard for you to tell a patient bad news. Over time, I feel like we've become friends, and I know you try very hard to do everything possible to help your patients."

It was a moment that stunned everyone in the room, particularly the other oncologist. She took me aside and told me, "Your mother is very special."

"I know," I said through the tears.

168 *The Guardian*

After the doctors left us alone, I apologized to my mom. I told her I wished I had been as good a daughter to her as she had been a mother to me. "Mom, I don't know what happened to me in the last few years since Megan and Dad died, but I just feel like I shut down. Like it was all too much. And that I let you down."

Then she gave me her understanding look of old that I knew so well. "Well, as a parent it is my job to take care of you," she said. "Not the other way around. To put you first." I didn't feel absolved, but I felt better having acknowledged my regrets. I hugged her repeatedly before I left and called her "my little mom." We laughed through the pain.

The next day, I resolved to start fresh. I wouldn't dwell on how quickly the end was coming or my shortcomings as a daughter or how much quality time I had missed. I would just enjoy the time remaining with my mom. I stopped in at the Dana-Farber gift shop before taking the elevator up to her room, and my eyes landed on two little stuffed lavender hippos with close-set black eyes. They were the kind of gift one usually buys for new babies—very plush and floppy and light. They were perfect.

My mom was sitting up in bed when I got there, trying but mostly failing to enjoy a heavily frosted cupcake—a special treat from the female oncologist we had met the day before—one small, determined bite at a time. One of the physical therapy aides smiled when she saw the hippos.

I bounded into her room with a big genuine smile, despite the heartbreak of the prior day. "Look what I found!" I announced. My mom and I had always loved collecting cuddly stuffed animals. "And they're purple" (my longtime favorite color). "I can keep one with me and you keep one, and that way, we can always have a source of comfort." My mom smiled and asked what we should name them. I let her do the honors, and she christened my hippo Lucy Belle (her nickname as a child) and her twin Lilly Poo.

Over the next few days, as my mom received and made phone calls, I noticed she kept telling people that although the cancer was terminal, she might have another two to three months left. She said she might even get stronger in hospice and have a short bounce-back period; maybe she would even be able to leave hospice and come home with me for a while. Based on Dr. K's reputation for professionalism and his unfaltering estimate of my mom's time remaining, I knew there was little to no chance of this happening. I reasoned that she needed to control her own narrative—as she had done with my homecoming story—even if it resulted in confusion for others.

The day of her transition to hospice, the medical team upgraded my mom's pain medication. After that, she declined rapidly, and I still ask myself: Did they know this would happen when they increased her dosage of Dilaudid? Or was this just a coincidence, and it was the cancer that robbed her of almost all her human qualities? The change in her personality and her impaired consciousness progressed so abruptly that in some ways it mirrored the way my dad left us.

The medical team explained to me that she could no longer be fed intravenously; long-term intravenous feeding was toxic, so either she ate or she didn't. But she couldn't digest food normally anymore, so I would be forced to watch my mother slowly starve to death.

For me, the following days were marked by more and more intimacy with her body. Although the hospice staff did the literal and figurative heavy lifting, I performed the small acts such as brushing my mom's teeth or rubbing her feet. Suddenly, we had switched places, and I was her caregiver. One day, I took a picture of her hands so I wouldn't forget what they looked like, even though mine were almost identical. It was one of the first things Jon noticed about my mother—the similarity of our long thin fingers.

But soon she began to experience touch as an assault. When the expert hospice staff moved her to change the bed linens or prop her up, she claimed they were manhandling her. One day I reached out to hold her hand and she shrieked, "Stop grabbing me!" It was impossible not to take this personally. It hurt to experience rejection from someone who had always been so generous with physical expressions of love. What I didn't know at the time is that when people are dying, their sensory input becomes distorted. As they start to let go of life, earthly touches may be perceived as holding

170   *The Guardian*

them back. Dying people also see and hear things that no one else does. My mom talked about seeing her mother and my father in the corners of her dim room.

I took short breaks to make phone calls or walk around the wooded hospice grounds if it wasn't too cold outside. I plugged my earbuds into my phone and listened to ballads that mirrored my misery. Again, Marvin Gaye was my intercessor, his voice transcendent as he sang the Beatles classic "Yesterday," asking the same question that was now confronting me: why did she have to go away?

I went through a panicky phase and obsessed about not being there when my mother died. Even then I knew this was a bit irrational, but I remembered my mother's story about Grandma Sylvia waiting until my mom had slipped out of her hospital room to pass away. One night, Jon and I went to eat at a nearby pizza place, and the plan was to go home afterward and get some rest. However, I was so gripped by the terror that she would die this particular night that we went back to the hospice and banged on the door until someone unlocked it and let us in. We stayed for another hour or so, and much to my surprise and relief, my mom was still alive the next day.

I'm guessing that my panic mirrored my mother's. Because of his work schedule, Jon could visit the hospice mainly on weekends and for a short time on weeknights when he came to pick me up. My mom would repeatedly ask for Jon when she was coherent enough to do so. She must have feared not having a chance to say good-bye.

We spent a depressed and abbreviated Thanksgiving at the hospice. We found my mom propped up at the central table in the dining room with another patient and her sons. She had insisted that the staff dress her (she wore a black Gucci Guilt T-shirt from her days selling men's fragrances) and transfer her to a wheelchair so she could partake in the holiday celebration. Although she managed to make some sarcastic quips, she looked frail and shrunken. I have a photograph of the three of us from that day. We form a pyramid, with Jon on top, smiling broadly in a black head warmer, and my mom on his left, leaning her head against mine. Her mouth is collapsed from both the weight loss and her missing dentures, and her eyes are unfocused, as if she is already in another place.

Her final days resembled our many car journeys over the years. When I was an infant, my mom used to drive me around in my car seat to settle me down and get me to sleep. To this day, I'm susceptible to dozing off in the passenger seat if the drive lasts more than an hour. When I was older, we would listen to her eclectic collection of tapes, her sunbaked left arm casually hanging out the car window. Jascha Heifetz's shtetl-tinged classical violin, Willie Nelson's country crooning, and Paul Simon's wistfully nostalgic poetry were all part of that looping soundtrack. To this day, all the songs from Simon's *Graceland* are etched into my gray matter.

I was no longer certain how much she could hear or understand during those last days, but I would clasp her hand and sing to her for hours on end—everything from musical theater like *Phantom of the Opera* to the maudlin but orchestrally lush Richard Harris version of "MacArthur Park" (my parents' favorite song) to the prayerful ballads of Roberta Flack. And, of course, lots of Paul Simon. Many of these songs formed the soundtrack of my parents' lives together. I sang to her because I knew that if anything could draw her out and bring her back to me, those songs could. When she recognized them, tears leaked from her mostly closed eyelids.

The last morning I spent with my mother, I arrived at the hospice to find one of her neighbors visiting. This was the first time I had met the woman, and she was obviously shocked by my mother's condition. When I looked down, I noticed giant salt crystals on my mother's brow. The only time I had seen salt like this was when Jon had run a marathon.

That afternoon, the hospice social worker came to visit me, and we talked about the idea of letting go. "I think people need to know that their loved ones are going to be okay without them. Maybe your mom is waiting because she's uncertain if that is true."

I couldn't say I disagreed with her premise. Given my mom's iron will and fierce loyalty, she probably wouldn't leave this earth until I released her. I had become increasingly anxious about her death, but that day was a turning point for me. How could she go

172   *The Guardian*

on like this? And why should she? I didn't know if it would make a difference, but before I left for the evening, I held my mom's hand and told her I would be okay. I told her to do what she felt was right, and if that meant letting go, so be it.

That night, Jon and I cooked dinner for the first time in weeks. We even shared a few laughs. It felt like forever since I had laughed. I went to sleep feeling strangely at peace. Early the next morning, coincidence or not, the hospice staff called to tell me that my mother had expired sometime before 6:00 a.m. She had received her so-called permission, and just as I knew she would, she had waited until she was alone to abandon the body that had become a sort of prison. I didn't go in for all that New Age language about transitions and journeys. My mother had died, as simple as that. The reality was as cold and hard and uncharming as her emaciated corpse, which I insisted on seeing and embracing one last time.

Liberty Crest

Three months after she died, we honored my mother's wishes and gave my parents an Arlington Cemetery homegoing, complete with a bugler, a firing party, and the folding and presentation of the American flag. What would Dad have thought of the pomp surrounding him on this day? On the one hand, he loved drama and theatrics. On the other hand, given his conflicting feelings about his naval service, he may have viewed it all through cynical and wearied eyes—too little, too late. I can imagine him tapping me on the shoulder in that rascally way of his and wisecracking, "Just take me out and shoot me." "But you're already dead, Dad," I'd retort.

Squeezed between the warmth and solidity of my two eldest sisters, I sobbed throughout the brief ceremony presided over by a Jewish chaplain. One white and one Black service member walked down the aisle cradling the heavy oak urn filled with two sets of ashes, a folded flag on top. Engraved on the urn were key lines from my parents' favorite song, "MacArthur Park"—lyrics invoking the "one" true love that persists throughout many years and relationships. Subsequently, a cortege wound its way to the niche wall where my parents would be laid to rest. My oldest sister took possession of the folded flag, handling it like a precious religious icon, and I was left feeling both bereft and somewhat relieved. So this, I thought, is the end.

But it wasn't. I still had many unanswered questions, and although I lacked a sense of resolution, I was determined to move on—until I happened to find my father's parole document. It was like a visitation from the past, urging me to pursue the truth. Consequently, six years after the Arlington service, I decided to see for myself what had become of Lorton, the place that had temporarily separated my father and me during my first days of life. On an unusually warm April day in 2022, I headed to Liberty Crest Village to view the vestiges of Lorton, fearing what I might find but knowing I had to confront whatever emotions the visit evoked.

The prison is surprisingly intact, despite its transformation into Liberty Crest Village. Much more than the bones of the institution are still present. On one side of the sprawling campus, the brick barracks have been transformed into the Workhouse Arts Center, which houses artist studios for ceramics, painting, theater, and film. The arcade that spans three sides of the quad might seem quaint to those ignorant of what it once signified. In the middle of the quad is a vibrantly colored LOVE sculpture (with a smaller "Virginia Is for Lovers" sign inside the letter *O*). I couldn't help but be reminded that the Commonwealth of Virginia had imprisoned and exiled Mildred and Richard Loving for expressing their love. In yet another eerie juxtaposition, historical markers and the Lucy Burns Museum tell the story of the prison and commemorate the suffering of imprisoned suffragists, including Anne Henrietta Martin, Elizabeth Selden Rogers, and Doris Stevens. These names represent just a few of the approximately 168 women arrested for picketing Woodrow Wilson's White House to show their support for women's voting rights. At Lorton, the suffragists were confined in the Occoquan Workhouse. On the night of November 14, 1917—known as the "Night of Terror"— the female prisoners were tortured and force-fed in an effort to break their hunger strike.

Looming on the distant horizon are guard towers and some abandoned brick buildings. I scrambled through a grassy field to get a closer look at one of the buildings, but there were no visible markers or signposts. I don't know what went on inside this Dickensian edifice with an industrial-sized drum outside it. Perhaps it was once a workhouse laundry.

Liberty Crest 175

On the opposite side of the campus, the original barracks have been renovated into apartments, one of which is still marked "9 Dorm Elderly." These residences were for more mature inmates— people like my father who were over the age of forty-three. Most of the men were thirty or younger, so at Lorton, my dad was considered an elder. What special challenges or privileges did that entail? Was this a means of protecting the older men or protecting the younger ones? Was there any separation between those convicted of violent crimes and so-called nonviolent offenders like my dad? (My brother Adrin reassured me that Dad would have been separated from the most violent offenders, although the Occoquan facility experienced its fair share of newsworthy violent outbreaks.[1]) I pondered these questions in the days after my visit, but while I was there, I was preoccupied by the idea of keeping the prison dormitory sign intact as some sort of demented set piece. Other extant signs included a prohibition on "unauthorized visiting in dormitories" and this warning: "Violaters subject to disciplinary action."

An otherwise attractive pool and lounge area is located behind barracks gates. I like a good read poolside, but I can't picture myself relaxing in such a triggering environment. As a Jew, I liken it to the Auschwitz motto: "Work sets you free." Most troubling is the massive guard tower that looms over the neutral-colored townhomes—a macabre and inescapable reminder of the history of this place, which was intended for neither leisure nor families. And yet this is where Adrin remembered seeing my father rubbing my mother's pregnant belly.

As I toured the site, paying my silent respects to it, oblivious young people played Frisbee in the shadow of the guard tower; a father and child whizzed by on their bikes. And as if the structures themselves don't create enough dissonance, the main thoroughfare in the development is christened Reformatory Way.

It was not lost on me that I saw mostly white residents on the grounds that day, although there were a few Black faces as well. For $500,000 (or more), you too can live in a townhome where mostly Black Washingtonians such as Chuck Brown, the Godfather of Go-Go (DC's original musical form) and singer of "The Numbers Game," had been incarcerated.

The site aroused a spectrum of emotions in me. I welcomed the informative plaques about suffragette history, and I appreciated the effort to bring art, beauty, and learning to a place of suffering. But I was also infuriated by the naming of the main street and the retention of prison signage, which trivialize incarceration. This aspect of Lorton has been Disneyfied, similar to the way some former Southern plantations have been transformed into popular marriage destinations. Some may argue that Lorton as an institution should be preserved because of its cultural significance, but I don't think this is the best and most effective means of preserving it or of encouraging citizens to address hard questions about mass incarceration, criminal justice reform, or systemic racism. The Lorton site could have become a vital teaching tool, along the lines of the Equal Justice Initiative's Legacy Museum in Montgomery, Alabama. It is situated on a site where Black people were once enslaved and covers the slavery era through mass incarceration. A companion site, the Freedom Monument Sculpture Park, uses contemporary artworks, first-person narratives, and historical artifacts to explore the lives of enslaved people.

Simultaneously, at Lorton I experienced something akin to the spiritual fulfillment that results from pilgrimage: I was present at the place where my father had been confined and where my mother had sacrificed and cared for him. In a way, I too had visited my father there, even before I emerged from my mother's body. In that sense, I was honoring both of their experiences. It was hallowed ground.

This last sentiment was ultimately the most resonant in the weeks and months subsequent to my visit. By seeking the truth, contextualizing my parents' lives, and coming full circle to Lorton, I freed myself. I now understood that my father's failings were more than merely individual shortcomings; they were also the failings of a society and its institutions, which were never intended to protect or nurture Black people. I recognized that my mother was not merely a victim but also a provider and a guardian. I knew that my life was part of theirs, but more importantly, it was also my own. I was astonished by their ability to endure and survive despite the hardships and the long odds. And they did it all so that I never had to face the same bleak choices.

Epilogue

Writing this memoir has allowed me to achieve a sense of equipoise. What my parents' deaths could not or would not transubstantiate, I accomplished by uncovering the truth—to the extent possible—about the circumstances surrounding a critical incident in their lives. My investigation, alongside a reexamination of my memories, enabled me to reclaim my father's humanity and recognize my mother's strength.

Since my 2022 visit to Liberty Crest, I learned that the Lucy Burns Museum now includes a permanent exhibit called "Counting the Days," which visualizes the experience of Lorton prisoners held in solitary confinement ("the Hole"). The exhibit was co-curated by documentarian Karim Mowatt, who served time in Lorton in the 1990s. Additionally, in early 2025, the museum hosted an exhibit called "Prison Reimagined," which narrates the story of mass incarceration from an insider's perspective. I am encouraged to learn about these efforts to spark dialogue about America's incarceration epidemic, and I hope that there are more opportunities to build on this type of thoughtful content for the public's benefit.

Crucial to my awakening was my engagement with historical records, beyond the parole document that sparked my curiosity and set me on this path. As I learned during my time in Alabama, documentation is key to an attorney's ability to weave a compelling mitigation story for a client. It is equally important in telling a family story. Curiously, a piece of paper with a previously undisclosed truth

178

Epilogue 179

has the power to bring you to your knees. This was certainly the case when I discovered the court disposition that exposed my mother's role in the numbers business. But it was also true for more peripheral family documents, such as my great-grandfather Seymour's death record. That document not only confirmed the names of my enslaved ancestors Martha and Frederick but also revealed that Christmas 1938 was a real turning point in my father's young life. In some ways, holding that piece of paper finally allowed me to see my father as a victim—an abandoned and abused child—and not just as a perpetrator. Othello's plea at the close of the play speaks to me deeply as a storyteller because it recognizes that what is left, after we are all merely dust and ashes, is the documentary evidence of our brief existence:

> I pray you, in your letters,
> When you shall these unlucky deeds relate,
> Speak of me as I am; nothing extenuate.[1]

Unfortunately, I hit many walls in my pursuit. I made a Freedom of Information Act (FOIA) request for any records related to my dad's sentence, but records from that time have been destroyed unless they were of "historical significance." I also made a FOIA request to the Department of Justice and the FBI for records back in 2021. In 2024 I received a letter informing me that "the FBI has located approximately 185 documents," but to date I am still waiting for this information to be processed.

In the early stages of my research, I was frequently plagued by doubt about the work I was undertaking. Was I betraying my parents' wishes or their confidences by writing about our family secrets? This doubt was put to rest by an evocative dream. Since my parents' passing, it is the only dream in which they both appear: I am in a room crammed with students sitting at long wooden benches as they pore over books and compare notes. I am distressed because I have two waist-high stacks of books that I somehow have to transport home. A call comes through an old-fashioned corded landline telephone. I shoulder the heavy black receiver as I answer

180   *Epilogue*

and hear my mother's voice. "Your dad is on his way to meet you," she says.

I anxiously respond, "Mom, I'm not ready yet. I still have hours of work to finish. And you know he doesn't like to wait."

"He will wait for you. It will be okay," she replies before abruptly hanging up.

I keep working, but I watch the door warily all the same. I can see that it is gently snowing outside. My father never bursts in and makes a scene, as I feared he would (and as he would have done in the waking world).

Only when I am finally finished studying does he walk through the door, dressed smartly in a black double-breasted coat and a fedora with a red feather. "Dad, I'm ready!" I greet him. "But I have all these books, and I don't know how we can carry them all in the snow."

He looks down at the two piles on the floor. He silently and deftly lifts one pile in each arm and then, through some sleight of hand, shuffles and condenses the books into one much smaller pile that we can easily divide. He gives me a few books and carries the rest himself.

We walk out into the night, side by side.

Acknowledgments

There are many people I would like to recognize for the roles they played in bringing this story to an audience. Thank you to the amazing team at the University Press of Kentucky for taking a chance on a first-time, unknown author. I am grateful to Mary Bisbee-Beek for playing matchmaker.

Along the way, Anne Dubuisson served as counsel, confidante, and therapist. I thank Anne for her close reading and attention.

Nicole Vorrasi Bates played a key role in tracking down my parents' legal files so that I could unearth previously unknown details. And my brother Johnny Matthews patiently answered my questions and helped fill in gaps in my information, including about how the street lottery worked.

Thank you to Bryan Stevenson for showing me that our world can be better and kinder and that our stories are worth telling.

I'm indebted to Assistant Professor Matthew Vaz for his scholarship on the street numbers and for suggesting some secondary sources.

Thank you to Lisa Crawley and the National Museum of African American History and Culture. I wasn't sure it would be possible to trace the family of Seymour Simms and uncover the names of my enslaved ancestors. I am grateful for Lisa's patience and determination.

Throughout the years I have had a lot of writing mentors who nurtured my love for the craft. They include Priscilla Alfandre, Kate Keller, Barbara Taylor, and Reuben Jackson.

Thank you to my longtime best friend Karima Barrow—thirty-five years and counting. It's hard to believe! Karima imagined me as a writer even before I could imagine it myself.

I am thankful that I reconnected with Michele Harper, a physician and writer I admire. She provided me with much-appreciated support and cheerleading during this process.

I am grateful to my sister Marilyn, who became a second mother to me in my time of loss. I love you.

Most of all, thank you to my husband, Jon, who is the greatest gift of all. He made sure I was well nourished and had a room of my own to pursue the hard work of writing, revising, researching, thinking, and crying. I am grateful for his grace, patience, humor, and empathy and for giving me a beautiful life. He also provided notes and comments on many, many drafts along the way. He is my hero. And he makes the best scrambled eggs.

Notes

The Lauryn Hill epigraph on page v is drawn from "NBA All-Star Weekend," West Hollywood, California, February 17, 2018, https://www.youtube.com/watch?v=-fDELNhTeZM.

Visiting Hours

1. Linda Wheeler, "No Escaping the History of Lorton Prison," *Washington Post*, February 6, 1999.

2. Christopher Solomon, "Lorton's Farm Team: Inmates Find Escape in Milking the Cows," *Washington Post*, October 19, 1995.

3. American Civil Liberties Union and Global Human Rights Clinic of the University of Chicago Law School, "Captive Labor: Exploitation of Incarcerated Workers," 2022, https://www.aclu.org/publications/captive-labor-exploitation-incarcerated-workers (accessed December 31, 2024).

4. Clint Smith, *How the Word Is Passed: A Reckoning with the History of Slavery across America* (New York: Little, Brown, 2021), 97.

The Investigation

1. John Kelly, "A New Film Explores the Life of Odessa Madre, the Queen of D.C.'s Underworld," *Washington Post*, October 12, 2021.

2. There are a few theories about the origins of the name we-sorts. "The most simple and plausible theory attributes the origins to the phrase, 'We sorts are not the same as you sorts,' which was employed by them in speaking to Negroes of the area. . . . It might be noted that the birth certificates and marriage licenses issued to these people generally have the race indicated as 'Colored-Wesort.'" Other theories attribute the name to the Algonquin term *witchott*, meaning oval house of bark, or the word *Wisoes*, referring to the

184　*Notes to Pages 16–26*

peace counselors of early Algonquin tribes. William Harlen Gilbert Jr., "The Wesorts of Southern Maryland: An Outcasted Group," *Journal of the Washington Academy of Sciences* 35, no. 8 (August 15, 1945).

Robeson testified before the House Un-American Activities Committee. Here is an excerpt:

> Mr. Arens: Are you now a member of the Communist Party?
>
> Mr. Robeson: Would you like to come to the ballot box when I vote and take out the ballot and see? . . . In Russia I felt for the first time like a full human being. No color prejudice like in Mississippi, no color prejudice like in Washington. It was the first time I felt like a human being. . . .
>
> Mr. Scherer: Why do you not stay in Russia?
>
> Mr. Robeson: Because my father was a slave, and my people died to build this country, and I am going to stay here, and have a part of it just like you. And no Fascist-minded people will drive me from it.

3. House Committee on Un-American Activities, *Investigation of the Unauthorized Use of U.S. Passports*, 84th Congress, part 3, June 12, 1956, in *Thirty Years of Treason: Excerpts from Hearings before the House Committee on Un-American Activities, 1938–1968*, ed. Eric Bentley (New York: Viking Press, 1971), 773–84, https://archive.org/stream/thirtyyearsoftreoounit/thirtyyearsoftreoounit _djvu.txt.

4. Oscar Hammerstein II and Jerome Kerns, "Ol' Man River," on *The Show Boat*, Brunswick 3766, 1928, 78 rpm, https://secondhandsongs.com /release/86019; Paul Robeson, "Ol' Man River," track 8 on *Paul Robeson Live at Carnegie Hall: The Historic May 9, 1958 Concert*, Vanguard Records, VMD 72020, 1990, compact disc. Coincidentally, this Carnegie Hall concert took place on my father's birthday.

5. Kelly, "New Film Explores the Life of Odessa Madre."

6. *United States of America v. Melvin Johnson, Sr., et al.*, appeal from the US District Court for the District of Columbia.

7. District court hearing, December 9, 1974.

8. Motion to reduce sentence, January 27, 1977.

The Lottery

1. Quoted in Matthew Vaz, *Running the Numbers: Race, Police, and the History of Urban Gambling* (Chicago: University of Chicago Press, 2020), 2.

2. John Meacham, *His Truth Is Marching On: John Lewis and the Power of Hope* (New York: Random House, 2020), 99.

Notes to Pages 27–33   185

3. The U Street neighborhood had one of DC's oldest Black banks. The Industrial Bank opened in 1934 and remained the only Black bank in Washington, DC, for at least two decades. Many Black people had the same experience when it came to white-owned lending institutions: they might have been allowed to deposit money, but they could not get a loan. The Industrial Bank financed loans for Black churches, Black businesses, and Black home buyers. It is still in existence, with numerous branches in offices of the Department of Motor Vehicles.

4. Les Payne, *The Dead Are Arising: The Life of Malcolm X* (New York: Liveright, 2020), 145.

5. Quoted in Joann Stevens, "Street 'Numbers' Already Popular," *Washington Post*, April 23, 1980.

Trouble Man

1. During my research, I discovered that Lizzie also had children outside of marriage at a young age—something none of my siblings seemed to know. In the 1910 census, Lizzie and Seymour were living with three young people identified as stepchildren: Alphonzo, age twelve; Annie, age ten; and William, age fifteen. Lizzie's marriage to Seymour was listed as her first, and the census taker noted that she had seven children, only six of them alive. Her three children with Seymour were identified as Isabel, age seven; Fred, age five; and Helen, age three.

2. Sherrilyn A. Ifill, *On the Courthouse Lawn: Confronting the Legacy of Lynching in the 21st Century*, rev. ed. (Boston: Beacon Press, 2018), 24–25. The Chesapeake Bay Bridge didn't span the bay until 1956.

3. Ifill, 30.

4. Armwood was lynched in 1933, but his story wasn't officially memorialized by the state of Maryland until 2019. Two years later, Maryland's governor pardoned Armwood for a crime he most likely didn't commit.

5. In some cases, trauma may be so great that it impairs the human capacity "to perceive, register, know, transmit, record and remember." This archaic survival response is based on ancient emotions related to real and perceived threats. Linda O'Neill, Tina Fraser, Andrew Kitchenham, and Verna McDonald, "Hidden Burdens: A Review of Intergenerational, Historical and Complex Trauma; Implications for Indigenous Families," *Journal of Child and Adolescent Trauma* 11, no. 2 (June 2018): 173–86.

6. One man had so deeply internalized the details of a lynching heard during family conversations that he "grew up believing he'd actually seen the lynching" himself. Ifill, *On the Courthouse Lawn*, xv.

7. Ifill, 21.

186 *Notes to Pages 34–59*

8. J. Samuel Walker, *Most of 14th Street Is Gone: The Washington, DC Riots of 1968* (New York: Oxford University Press, 2018), 12.

9. Briana Thomas, "The Forgotten History of U Street," *Washingtonian*, February 12, 2017.

10. The US Navy announced on April 7, 1942, that beginning June 1, Black men could enlist in general service rather than only the messman branch of the navy. This change was due to "pressure [that] converged on the Navy from several sources—the Army, the War Manpower Commission and the White House particularly—resulting in a great expansion of the Negro program." The program was considered a success: "On June 30, 1942, there were 5,026 Negroes in the regular Navy (almost all of them mess attendants); this figure was about two percent of the total enlisted male personnel of the Navy, and about two and one half percent of the male regulars. As of February 1, 1943, there were 26,909 Negroes in the Navy. Over two-thirds of these were messmen (18,227); 6,662 were General Service; 2,020 were Seabees. This represented about eight percent of the regular enlisted male personnel, and about two percent, again, of the total enlisted male personnel as of that date. The Negro program climbed rapidly in numbers. By December 31, 1943, there were 101,573 Negroes on active duty in various rates, 37,981 of whom were Stewards Mates (about 36%)." "The Negro in the Navy," US Naval Administration History of World War II #84, https: //www.history.navy.mil/research/library/online-reading-room/title-list-alphabetically/n/negro-navy-1947-adminhist84.html (accessed May 11, 2024).

11. "While 28 percent of white veterans attended college on the GI Bill, only 12 percent of Black veterans were able to use this benefit." Matthew F. Delmont, *Half American: The Epic Story of African Americans Fighting World War II at Home and Abroad* (New York: Viking, 2022), 269.

12. For instance, "in 1947, Black borrowers received only two of more than thirty-two hundred Veterans Administration–guaranteed home loans in Mississippi." Delmont, 267.

13. He is identified in the 1950 census as a printer laborer living with his first wife, Ruth, and my two oldest sisters on 4th Street NE. He was twenty-five years old at the time.

Code-Switching

1. Vernon C. Thompson, "Jack and Jill Chapters: The Top of the Hill for Black Professionals, " *Washington Post*, October 4, 1978.

Notes to Pages 67–75   187

Kingdom Come

1. Farah Karim-Cooper, *The Great White Bard: How to Love Shakespeare while Talking about Race* (New York: Viking, 2023), 133.

2. Black actors have struggled with the role of Othello. For instance, Hugh Quarshie poses: "If a black actor plays Othello does he not risk making racial stereotypes seem legitimate and even true? When a black actor plays a role written for a white actor in black make-up and for a predominately white audience, does he not encourage the white way, or rather the wrong way, of looking at black men, namely that black men, or 'Moors,' are over-emotional, excitable, and unstable." Karim-Cooper, 115.

3. "By Act 4 scene I, the torment is too much for Othello, when he hears Iago describe Cassio talk about Desdemona in his sleep. . . . Othello's emotional devolution is matched by a verbal one. This loss of English eloquence reinforces the racist dismissals of African speech in the period." Karim-Cooper, 127. However, it is significant that his innate eloquence is dislodged by a type of duress and subterfuge—it is racism and hatred that drive Othello to extremes.

4. Quoted in Paula Blackman, *Night Train to Nashville: The Greatest Untold Story of Music City* (Nashville: Harper Horizon, 2023), 156.

5. Kathryn Schultz, "Scratch That: What We've Lost Playing the Lottery," *New Yorker*, October 24, 2022.

6. John Mintz and Alfred E. Lewis, "Legal Games Don't Stop Trade: D.C. Numbers Racket Booms," *Washington Post*, April 26, 1983.

7. John Mintz, "Gambling Probe Leads to Arrest of 3 in D.C.," *Washington Post*, August 5, 1983.

8. Charles Babington and Ira Chinoy, "Lotteries Win with Slick Marketing," *Washington Post*, May 3, 1988.

9. Charles Babington and Ira Chinoy, "Lotteries Win with Slick Marketing," *Washington Post*, May 3, 1988.

10. Babington and Chinoy, "Lotteries Win with Slick Marketing."

11. Jonathan D. Cohen, *For a Dollar and a Dream: State Lotteries in Modern America* (New York: Oxford University Press, 2022), 158–59.

12. Chris Myers Asch and George Derek Musgrove, *Chocolate City: A History of Race and Democracy in the Nation's Capitol* (Chapel Hill: University of North Carolina Press, 2017), 401.

13. Cohen, *For a Dollar and a Dream*, 32.

14. Asch and Musrogve, *Chocolate City*, 239.

15. J. Samuel Walker, *Most of 14th Street Is Gone: The Washington, DC Riots of 1968* (New York: Oxford University Press, 2018), 99.

16. Quoted in Walker, 3.

17. Natalie Hopkinson, *Go-Go Live: The Musical Life and Death of a Chocolate City* (Durham, NC: Duke University Press Books, 2012), 21.

188   *Notes to Pages 75–90*

18. Advertisement, *Washington Post*, April 6, 1924, reproduced in "If Walls Could Talk: Tivoli Theater Was 'The Temple of the Arts,'" *Ghosts of DC* blog, April 16, 2012, https://ghostsofdc.org/2012/04/16/tivoli-theater-harry -crandall/.

19. Matthew Vaz, *Running the Numbers: Race, Police, and the History of Urban Gambling* (Chicago: University of Chicago Press, 2020), 150.

20. "Where Does Lottery Revenue Go?" ABC News, August 24, 2001, https://abcnews.go.com/US/story?id=92598&page=1; Valerie Strauss, "Mega-millions: Do Lotteries Really Benefit Public Schools?" *Washington Post*, March 30, 2012.

21. DC Lottery, "Where the Money Goes," https://dclottery.com/where -money-goes (accessed December 27, 2024).

22. Schultz, "Scratch That."

Insufficient Funds

1. William Shakespeare, *King Lear*, in *The Arden Shakespeare*, ed. R. A. Foakes (London: Bloomsbury, 2020), 79–80.

2. I have spelled this phonetically because I have never been able to locate the origins of this story.

3. The phrase itself, a protest against the abuse of power, has a rich history prior to its most infamous utterance. It allegedly dates from the days of the Roman Empire and Julius Caesar before becoming intimately linked to the new American republic.

4. Jill Lepore, "Gone with the Wind: In Pursuit of John Wilkes Booth," *New Yorker*, March 8, 2024.

5. Slavery was abolished by the third Maryland Constitution, which went into effect November 1, 1864.

6. It appears that my dad's grandfather, Seymour Simms, was the child of Frederick (b. 1823) and Martha (b. 1832). They and their five children are identified in the 1880 census. It is possible that the family of Frederick Semmes (as the name is spelled in the census) was part of the large estate of Anthony B. Semmes—a Charles County slave owner with $30,000 in personal property (enslaved people) and $25,000 in real estate. Like the Mudd family, the Semmes family was prominent in the area.

The Verdict

1. Rachel Louise Snyder, *No Visible Bruises: What We Don't Know about Domestic Violence Can Kill Us* (New York: Bloomsbury, 2019), 40.

2. Snyder, 145.

3. Snyder, 65–66.

Notes to Pages 95–122 189

4. For some reason, my father always misquoted Hamlet, omitting the word "only" following "cruel."

Evidence of Things Not Seen

1. Bryan Stevenson, *Just Mercy: A Story of Justice and Redemption* (New York: One World, 2015), 14.
2. The poetry in this chapter is mine.
3. Stevenson, *Just Mercy*, 17–18.
4. "A tornado in 1926 lifted an entire schoolhouse off its foundation. The school, which at the time contained 60 students and two teachers, was carried 50 feet away and blown into a grove of trees. When the schoolhouse struck the trees, it splintered to bits, killing 14 children. Some of the children were carried 500 feet, and one was found in the top of a tree more than 300 feet away. A desk from the school was found five miles away, and some of the wreckage was found in Upper Marlboro, 25 miles away. A page from the school register was found in Bowie, 36 miles away. The 1926 tornado killed a total of 16 people and injured about 40 others." Kevin Ambrose, "Remembering the La Plata Tornado, 15 Year Later," *Washington Post*, August 28, 2017. According to contemporaneous coverage of the tornado, at least two of the people killed were Black.
5. On his death certificate, Seymour Simms's cause of death is reported as generalized arteriosclerosis and coronary artery disease. His age is listed as sixty-seven, but depending on the source, his year of birth ranges from 1871 to 1874.
6. Virginia Ali, the octogenarian originator of Ben's Chili Bowl, a DC institution, later told me the same thing: "He was a gentleman, not a gangster." As another U Street old-timer, she had seen plenty of both types.

Graduation Day

1. William Shakespeare, *King Lear*, in *The Arden Shakespeare*, ed. R. A. Foakes (London: Bloomsbury, 2020), 253.

An Imperfect Mind

1. People who have been exposed to trauma in early life may experience age-related decline considerably earlier, and to a greater extent, than their nontraumatized counterparts. L. K. Lapp, C. Agbokou, and F. Ferreri, "PTSD in the Elderly: The Interaction between Trauma and Aging," *International Psychogeriatrics* 23, no. 6 (2011): 858–68.
2. William Shakespeare, *King Lear*, in *The Arden Shakespeare*, ed. R. A. Foakes (London: Bloomsbury, 2020), 264.

190 *Notes to Pages 130–179*

Probation

1. John Kelly, "In the Numbers Game of the 1950s, One Man Was on Top: 'Whitetop' Simpkins," *Washington Post*, February 27, 2021.

Two Weddings

1. *Snow White and the Seven Dwarfs*, the first full-length animated feature in motion picture history, debuted in 1937, the year before my mother was born. Snow White's dark hair was a departure for a movie heroine at the time.

2. My father was routinely mistaken as Ethiopian. DC has one of the largest communities of Ethiopian-born people in the United States.

3. Alvin's criminal career is chronicled in Chris Vogel, "Requiem for Bookie and Holocaust Survivor 'Alvin,'" *Washingtonian*, March 1, 2006.

4. William Shakespeare, *The Tragedy of Othello, the Moor of Venice*, ed. Barbara Mowatt and Paul Werstine (New York: Simon & Schuster, 2017), 41.

5. Farah Karim-Cooper, *The Great White Bard: How to Love Shakespeare while Talking about Race* (New York: Viking, 2023), 115.

6. Sources of trauma, including exposure to "community violence, domestic violence, sexual abuse, or terrorist attacks," can result in "long-lasting negative effects that extend well into adulthood. The direct effects may be psychological, behavioral, social, and even biological." Phelan Wyrick and Kadee Atkinson, "Examining the Relationship between Childhood Trauma and Involvement in the Justice System," *National Institute of Justice Journal*, https://nij.ojp.gov/topics/articles/examining-relationship-between-childhood-trauma-and-involvement-justice-system (accessed May 27, 2024).

Liberty Crest

1. "The dormitories where older inmates live are generally quieter and better kept than the others. Residents often spend a large part of their day reading and sleeping. There is not much loud radio playing and usually the youngest of the older inmates stands watch at the entrance to discourage the 'riffraff,' as troublemakers are called." Courtland Milloy, "The Elders of Lorton," *Washington Post*, April 13, 1982.

Epilogue

1. William Shakespeare, *The Tragedy of Othello, the Moor of Venice*, ed. Barbara Mowatt and Paul Werstine (New York: Simon & Schuster, 2017), 263.

Selected Bibliography

American Civil Liberties Union and Global Human Rights Clinic of the University of Chicago Law School. "Captive Labor: Exploitation of Incarcerated Workers." 2022. https://www.aclu.org/publications/captive-labor-exploitation-incarcerated-workers.

Asch, Chris Myers, and George Derek Musgrove. *Chocolate City: A History of Race and Democracy in the Nation's Capitol.* Chapel Hill: University of North Carolina Press, 2017.

Blackman, Paula. *Night Train to Nashville: The Greatest Untold Story of Music City.* Nashville: Harper Horizon, 2023.

Bredemier, Kenneth. "D.C. Lottery One of the Most Expensive." *Washington Post,* February 3, 1983.

Cohen, Jonathan D. *For a Dollar and a Dream: State Lotteries in Modern America.* New York: Oxford University Press, 2022.

Delmont, Matthew F. *Half American: The Epic Story of African Americans Fighting World War II at Home and Abroad.* New York: Viking, 2022.

Gilbert, William Harlen, Jr. "The Wesorts of Southern Maryland: An Outcasted Group." *Journal of the Washington Academy of Sciences* 35, no. 8 (August 15, 1945).

Hopkinson, Natalie. *Go-Go Live: The Musical Life and Death of a Chocolate City.* Durham, NC: Duke University Press Books, 2012.

Ifill, Sherrilyn A. *On the Courthouse Lawn: Confronting the Legacy of Lynching in the 21st Century.* Rev. ed. Boston: Beacon Press, 2018.

Karim-Cooper, Farah. *The Great White Bard: How to Love Shakespeare while Talking about Race.* New York: Viking, 2023.

Lapp, L. K., C. Agbokou, and F. Ferreri. "PTSD in the Elderly: The Interaction between Trauma and Aging." *International Psychogeriatrics* 23, no. 6 (2011): 858–68.

Selected Bibliography

Meacham, John. *His Truth Is Marching On: John Lewis and the Power of Hope.* New York: Random House, 2020.

Mintz, John. "Gambling Probe Leads to Arrest of 3 in D.C." *Washington Post,* August 5, 1983.

"The Negro in the Navy." US Naval Administration History of World War II #84. https://www.history.navy.mil/research/library/online-reading-room /title-list-alphabetically/n/negro-navy-1947-adminhist84.html. Accessed May 11, 2024.

O'Neill, Linda, Tina Fraser, Andrew Kitchenham, and Verna McDonald. "Hidden Burdens: A Review of Intergenerational, Historical and Complex Trauma; Implications for Indigenous Families." *Journal of Child and Adolescent Trauma* 11, no. 2 (June 2018): 173–86.

Payne, Les. *The Dead Are Arising: The Life of Malcolm X.* New York: Liveright, 2020.

Schultz, Kathryn. "Scratch That: What We've Lost Playing the Lottery." *New Yorker,* October 24, 2022.

Shakespeare, William. *King Lear.* In *The Arden Shakespeare,* edited by R. A. Foakes. London: Bloomsbury, 2020.

———. *Richard III.* Edited by Barbara Mowatt and Paul Werstine. New York: Simon & Schuster, 2018.

———. *The Tragedy of Othello, the Moor of Venice.* Edited by Barbara Mowatt and Paul Werstine. New York: Simon & Schuster, 2017.

Smith, Clint. *How the Word Is Passed: A Reckoning with the History of Slavery across America.* New York: Little, Brown, 2021.

Snyder, Rachel Louise. *No Visible Bruises: What We Don't Know about Domestic Violence Can Kill Us.* New York: Bloomsbury, 2019.

Solomon, Christopher. "Lorton's Farm Team: Inmates Find Escape in Milking the Cows." *Washington Post,* October 19, 1995.

Stevenson, Bryan. *Just Mercy: A Story of Justice and Redemption.* New York: One World, 2015.

Vaz, Matthew. *Running the Numbers: Race, Police, and the History of Urban Gambling.* Chicago: University of Chicago Press, 2020.

Walker, J. Samuel. *Most of 14th Street Is Gone: The Washington, DC Riots of 1968.* New York: Oxford University Press, 2018.

Wheeler, Linda. "No Escaping the History of Lorton Prison." *Washington Post,* February 6, 1999.

Wyrick, Phelan, and Kadee Atkinson. "Examining the Relationship between Childhood Trauma and Involvement in the Justice System." *National Institute of Justice Journal.* https://nij.ojp.gov/topics/articles/examining -relationship-between-childhood-trauma-and-involvement-justice-system. Accessed May 27, 2024.